STUDIES IN GERMAN LITERATURE No. 5

General Editors

L. W. Forster, Professor of German,

and

B. A. Rowley, Lecturer in German,
University College, London

EICHENDORFF:
AUS DEM LEBEN EINES
TAUGENICHTS

by

G. T. HUGHES

Lecturer in Comparative Literary Studies
University of Manchester

BARRON'S EDUCATIONAL SERIES, INC.
Great Neck, New York

© *G. T. Hughes 1961*

First published 1961

Library of Congress Catalogue Card Number: 62-20074
Printed in the United States of America

Contents

1. Reception

Huck Finn on the Mississippi and the Taugenichts on the road to Rome – these innocent picaros have grown into the fabric of the national dream. The American ideal seems revolutionary and self-reliant; the German nostalgic and magical.

Aus dem Leben eines Taugenichts is a curious amalgam of fairy-tale, pilgrim's progress and picaresque narrative; the innocent abroad in a providential world comes through all his adventures unscathed and wins the hand of the nebulous fair lady. Within this framework there is an artistic construct of much subtlety and rich symbolic significance, not to be exhausted by the commonplaces of national character or literary school. The rhetoric of nationality belongs to the hustings rather than to literary criticism, and classifications into 'Romantic', 'Realist' and the like are more often useful signposts than adequate commentary on a piece of literature. Yet it is in terms of its 'German' or 'Romantic' qualities that the *Taugenichts* has all too frequently been presented in its homeland. The harmless figure of the Taugenichts himself becomes the chiming-glass of the German temperament and stumbles out of the book towards tragedy. Somnambulistic and non-violent, he forms the childlike ideal of middle-aged and sometimes ruthless men, and a tortured and complex race finds its longing for simplicity and directness satisfied in him.

'Er ist Volk,' wrote Thomas Mann in 1916, taking him as a weapon in the ideological struggle, 'Er ist die Reinheit des Volksliedes und des Märchens und also gesund und nicht exzentrisch...'; and he goes on to call him 'ein in seiner Anspruchslosigkeit rührendes und erheiterndes Symbol reiner Menschlichkeit, human-romantischer Menschlichkeit, noch einmal denn: des deutschen Menschen' (*Betrachtungen eines Unpolitischen*, Berlin, 1920, pp. 372ff). Examples of this interpretation could be multiplied, but let two at a hundred years interval do duty for all:

... der *Taugenichts* ist after all nicht mehr und nicht weniger als eine Verkörperung des deutschen Gemüts, die liebenswürdige Type nicht eines Standes bloss, sondern einer ganzen Nation. Kein andres Volk hat solch Buch. Ein Buch aber, in dem sich vor einem, auf wenigen Blättern und mit der Naivität eines Märchens, die tiefsten Seiten unseres Lebens erschliessen, ein solches Buch muss was Apartes sein. (Letter of Fontane to Paul Heyse, 6 January 1857)

Mit dem Taugenichts hat Eichendorff den deutschen Mann, in ewige Jugend verzaubert, ... vor uns hingestellt, und alles, was wir als deutsch empfinden, ist in diesen zehn Kapiteln gesagt und gesungen. (W. Köhler, 1957, p. 195)

This is not, of course, to say that all German critics have received the tale with enthusiasm; a good deal of reserve is evident among the nineteenth-century historians of literature, who tended to find it charming but not serious-minded enough. Hermann Palm in the Eichendorff article in the *Allgemeine deutsche Biographie* (1877) puts it bluntly:

Die gerühmteste seiner Novellen *Aus dem Leben eines Taugenichts*... [mag allerdings] durch die Schilderung des vergnügten zwecklosen Umhertreibens ihres Helden in der Welt auf eine gleichgestimmte Jugend noch heute einen behaglichen Eindruck machen; den ernsten Leser werden nur die zum Teil trefflichen eingestreuten Lieder fesseln, während die an seine Phantasie gestellten Zumutungen allenthalben den Eindruck stören.

These were, however, minority reports, and its popularity is sufficiently attested by the number of editions into which it has run: at a rough estimate 96 between 1826 and 1925 and 58 between 1945 and 1954. The view of the common man seems to have been very much that of the *Nordwestdeutsche Zeitung* (quoted on Eichendorff's 150th birthday in 1938: *Aurora*, VIII): 'Ein trefflich gezeichnetes Bild herzerfrischender deutscher Art, dem die Zeit, in der Eichendorff es schuf, ein romantisches Gewand verlieh.' Thus, however we may read the *Taugenichts*, we must not forget how generations of Germans have read it, and what sense of national identification with it they have achieved.

Outside Germany, in fact, despite numerous translations, it

has seemed to lack something and has not really made its mark; though the lack of enthusiasm has rarely been as complete as in the early notice in the *Atlantic Monthly* (anonymous review of Leland's translation, vol. XVIII, no. 106, August 1866):

> ... its leading qualities of fanciful incoherency and unbridled feebleness..., being translated into our pitiless English, its poverty of wit and feeling and imagination is apparent; and one is soon weary of its mere fantasticality.

The recent translation by B. Q. Morgan (London, 1955) was given a mildly approving notice in the *Times Literary Supplement* (23 December 1955) but otherwise attracted very little attention.

Both within Germany and outside it, however, the popular image of the *Taugenichts* has included one other feature: it is the quintessence of romanticism. The term 'romanticism', with or without a capital, is nowadays viewed with some justifiable suspicion. There is always the danger, when using the terminology of literary schools, of implying a much greater degree of common awareness and unity of purpose than was present in the minds of the authors themselves; and this leads to the even greater distortion of making the author just a piece in a mosaic. This is not to say that such terms are meaningless. Romanticism did have a conscious contemporary programme; one has only to recall Friedrich Schlegel's influence to recognize that the movement had a theoretical basis. Equally there is a sense in which certain motifs and attitudes can be associated with a group of writers in the first twenty or thirty years of the nineteenth century and connected with the theories of the Romantic programme. In both these ways the term 'Romanticism' is superior to the more completely artificial concepts like 'Biedermeier' or 'Poetic Realism'; and it should be possible to make some approach to precision by adopting more widely the convention of using 'Romantic' to connote some degree of conscious conformity with the purposes of the theorists, and 'romantic' as the more general word for the collectivity of motifs and themes.

But the all too frequent procedure in the chattier kind of

German criticism has been to take it for granted that everyone is agreed about what Romanticism is, and then to show how admirably the *Taugenichts* fits in to the non-existent definition. (On a slightly more sophisticated level this is really all that Schumann, 1936, does.)

A representative selection of such judgements is given by Gould (1934), who, claiming Walzel as a predecessor, argues that the *Novelle* is in fact a satire on Romanticism. He bases his case on Eichendorff's supposed satirizing of Romantic writers elsewhere – including *Ahnung und Gegenwart* – and on the comic presentation of primitivism in the *Taugenichts*. He finds that the Romantic glorification of purposelessness and impulse is everywhere held up to ridicule, as is the Romantic view of the common people, whose songs, proverbs, crudities and lack of refinement are shown up for what they are. Feise (1936/1950) seeks to controvert these propositions by pointing out that Eichendorff was himself steeped in the folk-song tradition, and by asking why he presented his hero with such evident delight if his purpose was to attack the Romantic conception of the folk as embodied in the Taugenichts.

Gould's arguments collapse under the weight of their exaggerations; they ignore the general mood of the work and the effect on the narrative tone of the use of the Taugenichts as the narrator. Nor does it occur to him to ask why Eichendorff's contemporaries failed to recognize the satire on primitivism. Gould's excesses apart, however, it is now generally accepted by critics that there is room for considerable modification of the view that the *Taugenichts* represents the pure distillation of the Romantic movement (cf. R. Tymms, *German Romantic Literature*, London, 1955).

The details of the young Eichendorff's contacts with the figures of the movement have been sharply disputed (the latest and best account is that by Möbus, 1954), but is it clear that his relationship with Romanticism was far from simple and clear-cut. Admiration for Arnim and Brentano and for Görres' symbolic view of poetry, an ambivalent attitude towards

Friedrich Schlegel, and the reversal somewhere between about 1809 and 1811 of his youthful attraction to the windy enthusiasms of Otto Heinrich Graf von Loeben, mark various stages in his development.

There is, of course, considerable danger of falsification in reading back into his formative period the formulations he later arrived at in his own survey of German literature, the *Geschichte der poetischen Literatur Deutschlands* of 1857, but taken together with the internal evidence of the creative works and the sparse details of letters and diaries they do help to suggest the direction of his dissatisfaction. Romanticism had too often become frivolously stylized; it had sometimes become so ethereal as to lose contact with life without establishing its contact with heaven, for religion had come to be used merely in the service of art:

> Sie [the later Romantics] hatten die Phantasie von den Banden des Verstandes gelöst; aber die Befreite war ihnen plötzlich davongefahren und über Gipfel und Wipfel in wüstem Flug bis in jenes unwirtbare Leer hinausgestürzt, wo der Himmel dunkel und die Erde nur noch in gespensterhafter Luftspiegelung erscheint. *(Poetische Literatur,* II, 186-7)

Keller (1954) may be consulted for Eichendorff's attitude towards Romanticism generally, though he does not mention Gould's article, nor does he deal with the *Taugenichts*.

The motifs, the vocabulary, the intellectual background of the Romantic movement were still very much alive for Eichendorff in the years in which he was writing the *Taugenichts* – as indeed *Das Marmorbild,* completed not long before, abundantly testifies. But there was also a good deal with which he had lost patience. Disenchantment with the stylizations of late Romanticism is clearly visible in the lengthy and contextually irrelevant tableau in Chapter Eight of the *Taugenichts,* with its explicit allusion to the opening paragraphs of E.T.A. Hoffmann's tale *Die Fermate :*

> 'Barbar!... du rennst da mitten in das sinnreiche Tableau von der schönen Beschreibung hinein, welche der selige Hoffmann, Seite 347 des *Frauentaschenbuches für 1816,* von dem schönsten Hummelschen

Bilde gibt, das im Herbste 1814 auf der Berliner Kunstausstellung zu sehen war!'

Eichendorff's attitude to Hoffmann grew naturally out of his moral disapproval: 'Sein ganzes Leben war im Grunde nur ein geistreiches Capriccio ohne eigentlichen Inhalt' *(Poetische Literatur*, II, 191). But here it is the artificiality of his art that is pointed by the content (implied imitation and ostentation) and the puns (Silberblick, goldener Faden, and especially Schätze) of the paragraph immediately following the Hoffmann-Hummel reference:

> 'Ach was!' entgegnete der junge Mann, 'mit euren Tableaus von Tableaus! Mein selbsterfundenes Bild für die andern und mein Mädchen für mich allein! So will ich es halten! O du Ungetreue, du Falsche!' fuhr er dann von neuem gegen das arme Mädchen fort, 'du kritische Seele, die in der Malerkunst nur den Silberblick und in der Dichtkunst nur den goldenen Faden sucht, und keinen Liebsten, sondern nur lauter Schätze hat!...'

This strange, intrusive scene in the *Taugenichts* suggests that Eichendorff felt a compulsion to dissociate himself from some of the artificial aspects of late Romanticism. Possibly the uncharacteristically precise reference to the *Frauentaschenbuch für 1816* is motivated by the fact that he had himself published seven poems in that particular volume (including 'Lass mich ein, mein süsses Schätzchen') and that he did not, on reflection, care for the company he was keeping.

There has also been some discussion of the *Taugenichts* as representing the transformation of Romanticism into Biedermeier, with the suggestion that, from the 1820s on, Eichendorff lies on the border between the two (Kohlschmidt, 1950/55). The main planks of the argument are that Eichendorff's works now reveal a lack of tension and a modified subjectivism, which are both uncharacteristic of Romanticism. Wiese (1956), however, rejects the claim that the *Taugenichts* is a product of the Biedermeier imagination; the mood, the lyricism are against it; the world still does not exist in its own right but depends on the human soul.

But these are all sophisticated questionings. The popular imagination has no doubt about the Romantic character of the *Taugenichts;* for the school editions the equations are simple. In the series *Dr. Wilhelm Königs Erläuterungen zu den Klassikern,* for instance, Schuldirektor Richard Stecher ('nach Dr. Josef Lackner') calls it Romantic by virtue of eight qualities: the character of the Taugenichts himself, the students, the interspersed songs, the unforced behaviour of the characters, the animistic aspects of nature, the imprecision of locality, the evocation of particular moods, and the occurrence of the mysterious or ghostly. That the *Taugenichts* is full of such romantic motifs is, as will become clear, not in dispute. But it is a much more independent production than a listing of derivative elements of this kind implies; it was written by Eichendorff, not by the Romantic movement.

A formal history of the reception of *Aus dem Leben eines Taugenichts* would show other elements assuming importance from time to time; one of the latest interpretations is predominantly social (Lukács, 1940/52). But the labels that cover the surface of the *Novelle* are Germanic and Romantic; these are the faded tickets of its fame. The present attempt at an interpretation will suggest that these features were not mainly what inspired Eichendorff, and that they are not those of most interest to readers now. The *Taugenichts* is much more than their sum, but perhaps less than their extremes. In it the childlike agent of the human condition shines as he does in *Huckleberry Finn.*

2. Genesis

Ich habe durch langes, nur zu oft scheinbar zweckloses, Umhertreiben im Leben einen weiten Umkreis von Aussichten gewonnen, aus deren Gemisch von Zauber, lächerlicher Dummheit, Freude und Scherz ich mich manchmal kaum herauswinden kann, und eine unwiderstehliche Lust dabei, gerade nur das alles, was ich gesehen, gehört und durchlebt, einmal recht keck und deutlich zu frommer Ergötzung wieder darzustellen.

This extract from a letter to Fouqué, dated Breslau 15 June 1816, is regarded by Appelt (1928) as being without a doubt Eichendorff's first reference to *Aus dem Leben eines Taugenichts*, and its content could certainly suggest this, though it is difficult to see that there is anything to exclude the possibility of its referring to *Das Marmorbild* or to *Krieg den Philistern*. There is, however, one other piece of evidence to support an early dating of the *Taugenichts*. A note from a MS sheet then (1923) in the possession of Karl von Eichendorff is quoted by the editors of the poems in the collected works (*SW*, I, ii, 640):

> Jetzt früh immer, wie ich gerade Lust habe, mein Marmorbild abschreiben und den Taugenichts beendigen!

The sheet is not dated, but a second note on it refers to a communication for the Prussian Chancellor Hardenberg that is clearly the one mentioned in a letter by Joseph's brother Wilhelm on 15 October 1817.

What course work on the *Novelle* then followed is by no means clear, and perhaps it never will be; though it is known (*Jahrbuch der neueren deutschen Literatur*, N.S., II, 1922, 84) that some relevant material is being held back for the collected edition – the *Märchen und Novellen* are to form volume V, edited by H. Kunisch. Most of the letters from this creative period seem, however, to have been irretrievably lost.

In 1823 'Ein Kapitel aus dem Leben eines Taugenichts' was published in numbers 152 to 158 of the *Deutsche Blätter* edited by Holtei, Schall and Barth. This represented the first chapter as we now have it, but it is not known whether the *Novelle* as a whole was already finished or whether this was all that had been written. It is, however, generally assumed (e.g. by Schulhof and Sauer, *SW*, I, ii, 659) that the later chapters were either written or revised after 1820. The main evidence for this lies in the belief that the song of the Prague students in Chapter Nine was inspired by Wilhelm Müller's three 'Prager Musikant' poems in his *Gedichte aus den hinterlassenen Papieren eines reisenden Waldhornisten* (1820). There is also the reference to 'der selige

Hoffmann' (E.T.A. Hoffmann died in 1822). Neither point is particularly strong. Appelt gives a number of reasons for doubting the Müller inspiration, the most potent being that the similarity is confined to the title, and the Hoffmann reference could obviously have been a simple emendation. A draft in the Sedlnitz MSS called by Eichendorff 'Familiengemälde' and corresponding to the second chapter of the *Taugenichts* is, apparently, of no help in dating the work. (It may be added that the whereabouts of these MSS is not now clear. They must either be in the possession of the publishers of the collected works or have been lost in the destruction of the Eichendorff Museum at Neisse during the Russian advance in 1945.)

The most one can say, therefore, is that it seems reasonable to suppose that Eichendorff worked at his *Novelle* during the early 1820s, whether completing it or revising it cannot be determined, though it is pertinent to note that a good deal of revision did take place sometime (see below). Brandenburg (1922) and the even less meticulous Köhler (1957) categorically support the legend that the *Taugenichts* was written at Schloss Silberhammer near Danzig. This may indeed well be so, but there is no evidence to prove it; and speculation as to the suitability of the scene as a background for the *Novelle* remains pure speculation.

The state of the MS, as far as it is available, does allow of some deductions about the way Eichendorff went to work on the *Taugenichts*, even if it does not make positive dating possible. Parts of the MS of the original (?) draft of the *Novelle* have been fairly frequently reproduced (cf. Köhler, 1957, plate 24, the first page: *SW*, XXII, 48, the first two pages: A. Jahn, 1939, twenty pages; see also the Cotta edition, IV, 1958, 1493–1511, *Der neue Troubadour*). From these it can be seen that corrections are relatively frequent and that, though they are mainly slight emendations of inelegancies, they do also suggest that Eichendorff was not yet wholly certain of the tone of the *Novelle*. One example must suffice. On the second page we read:

Ich rief den armen Leuten nach allen Seiten [recht stolz und zufrieden] Adjes zu...

The deleted phrase is, however, restored in the text as we have it, and is pretty much in character with the Taugenichts as he is eventually portrayed. The first page has written along one side: 'NB Das Ganze ehe ichs abschreiben lasse noch vorher durch-korrigieren'; and the discrepancies between the corrected text of the MS facsimile and the first edition indicate that this process of further revision was also carried out.[1]

Aus dem Leben eines Taugenichts und das Marmorbild. Zwei Novellen nebst einem Anhang von Liedern und Romanzen was eventually published in 1826 by the Vereinsbuchhandlung, Berlin, and the *Taugenichts* was included in part IV of his collected works, Berlin, Simion, 1841/2. Later editions, Leipzig, Voigt and Günther, 1864 and Leipzig, Amelang, 1883, introduced many variants, most of them obvious printer's errors. (A few of these variants are shown in the notes to Müller, *Entwicklungsreihe*, 1936, though even this is not a reliable critical edition.) From this short account of the state of the MS and of the various texts of the *Taugenichts* it will be clear that our knowledge of its genesis, and of Eichendorff's detailed intentions in it, must remain to some extent incomplete until a proper critical edition appears.

One further point can, however, be made. Eichendorff found much difficulty in choosing a title, as had been the case a few years before with *Ahnung und Gegenwart*. Here again the facsimile of the first page of the MS provides the evidence, and it has been assumed (cf. Appelt) that some four variants can be found in it. But it seems more likely, when one looks at the pattern of the page-heading, that there are really only two: 'Zwei Kapitel aus dem Leben eines armen Taugenichts/Oder der moderne Troubadour', which was then changed to 'Der neue Troubadour/Ein Kapitel aus dem Leben eines armen Taugenichts; mitgetheilt durch J. Frhr. v. E.' The final dropping of 'arm' can perhaps be explained in terms of the development of

[1] I am indebted to Professor R. E. Keller for suggestions about the interpretation of the MS.

the *Novelle*. Things do not by any means go ill with the Taugenichts, and it would have been a false note to suggest misfortune
in the title; his original circumstances cast no gloom on his path.
And as for 'Troubadour', it appears in *Die Freier* to have acquired
a half-pejorative meaning for Eichendorff; this he would not
have wanted for the Taugenichts. We may also conclude from
the dropping of this term that a possible development of the
artistic side of the hero, the Taugenichts as a representative of the
artistic personality, gave way to an interest in him as anti-
Philistine, a non-bourgeois, an innocent benefiary of providence,
a living testimony to the sixth chapter of St. Matthew.

Autobiography.

The letter to Fouqué quoted at the beginning of this chapter, if
indeed it refers to the *Taugenichts*, implies a close connexion
between the genesis of the *Novelle* and the events of Eichendorff's
own life. This autobiographical aspect has been investigated by a
number of writers, notably Appelt (1928). Some of the details
are not helpful: we are told that drunken persons appear both
in the *Novelle* and in the diaries, that Eichendorff liked going to
the theatre and that there are theatrical elements in the *Taugenichts*, that dancing peasants are frequently mentioned in the
diaries, that the young Eichendorff used to climb trees as the
Taugenichts does. (Rather more plausible, but still very minor,
resemblances between the *Novelle* and the diaries are listed in
Sucher's edition, 1929, pp. xxxiii–xl.) More to the point are
the references to the experiences of his journey on the Danube
from Regensburg to Vienna in 1808, to the enrichment of his
feeling for landscape by his stay in Vienna, 1810–1813, and to
his longing for his Silesian home during his years in Danzig,
1821–1824, and Königsberg, 1824–1831, though in this case the
dates suggest a need for caution. A stronger point might have
been the death of his father in 1818, and of his mother in 1821,
with the consequent loss of Lubowitz.

It is scarcely fruitful to search through *Aus dem Leben eines
Taugenichts* for detailed correspondences to Eichendorff's life;

this is no *Ulysses*. The impetus is one of mood rather than detail. One might instance the rococo atmosphere of Schloss Lubowitz, or 'die frischen Wälder von Oberschlesien' (letter of 1815 to Philipp Veit, *SW*, XII, 15), or Heidelberg,

> wo... der Waldhauch von den Bergen erfrischend durch die Strassen ging und nachts die Brunnen auf den stillen Plätzen rauschten, und in dem Blütenmeer der Gärten rings die Nachtigallen schlugen, mitten zwischen Burgen und Erinnerungen einer grossen Vergangenheit; da atmete auch der Student freier auf und schämte vor der ernsten Sagenwelt sich der kleinlichen Brotjägerei und der kindischen Brutalität. *(Halle und Heidelberg)*

or Vienna, where

> [Friedrich] Schlegel sitzt recht wie ein deutscher Künstler hinter dem gedekten mit Brodten belegten Tische mit ihr, wie auf alten Bildern, u. ist unbeschreiblich heiter und liebenswürdig. Torte, Braten, Wein, Punsch. Philipp [Veit] singt Lieder, wozu Eggers Guitarre spielt, Körner singt u. spielt durch dick u. dünn Lieder aus des Knaben Wunderhorn u. Burschenlieder... (diary entry of 13 February 1812, *SW*, XI, 308–9)

It is out of mood-pictures such as these, rising up out of the past, that much of the *Taugenichts* is composed, and the conditions under which they were evoked is suggested by another letter to Fouqué, this time certainly with reference to *Das Marmorbild*:

> Da mir nunmehr die Gegenwart in tausend verdriesslichen... Geschäften in eine fast lächerliche Nähe gerückt ist, ... so habe ich in vorliegendem Märchen versucht, mich in die Vergangenheit und in einem fremden Himmelsstrich zu flüchten, und betrachte dasselbe als einen Spaziergang in amtsfreien Stunden ins Freie hinaus. (2 December 1817)

Sources.

The search for other sources need not detain us long. 'Eichendorff lui-même: voilà l'unique 'source' ', says Sucher (1929, p. xxxiv) and this is only a slight exaggeration.

In addition to the passages from diaries and letters that throw light on the moods, if not particularly on the details, of the

Taugenichts, many individual motifs derive from *Ahnung und Gegenwart* or the poems. These were both the product of personal experience and, in many cases, the common property of the Romantic movement. Eichendorff sometimes quotes directly from himself (see Kohlschmidt, 1955, for examples) but more often in the later works, particularly in *Dichter und ihre Gesellen*. One minor instance of this kind in the *Taugenichts* may however be noted: the echo of 'Den lieben Gott lass in dir walten' from *Ahnung und Gegenwart (SW*, III, 332).

A source in Slav tales for the story of the miller and his son has been suggested by T. Ibing *(Das Verhältnis des Dichters Freiherrn J. v. Eichendorff zu Volksbrauch, Aberglaube, Sage und Märchen. Eine Quellenuntersuchung*, Bonn, 1912) but is scorned by Sucher. And indeed it seems scarcely necessary to look so far and to bring Eichendorff's knowledge of Polish into play. Of writers whom Eichendorff much admired, Grimmelshausen (see Rehder, 1957) and Jean Paul will have contributed something to the *Taugenichts;* but some of the other names suggested seem wide of the mark. Heinse's *Ardinghello* was a novel of which he had, in later years at any rate, a very poor opinion; nor did he think any more highly of J. M. Miller's *Siegwart* from which Hilda Schulhof *(Euphorion*, XXIII, 1921, 109–110 and *SW*, I, ii, 728) supposes him, on the basis of some very thin parallels, to have taken the motif of the lovelorn gardener as well as some phrases in the lyrics.

One more serious possibility remains: Arnim's essay 'Von Volksliedern' prefaced to the first volume of *Des Knaben Wunderhorn*, 1805. Möbus (1954, p. 29) quotes from this essay a passage describing how the life of the common people had through the ages become less joyous, more purposive; the working-class had come to have needs which had to be met by factories and more workers:

> so wurde jeder als Taugenichts verbannt, der umherschwärmte in unbestimmtem Geschäfte, als wenn dem Staate und der Welt nicht gerade diese schwärmenden Landsknechte und irrenden Ritter, diese ewige Völkerwanderung ohne Grenzverrückung, diese wandernde

Universität und Kunstverbrüderung zu seinen besten schwierigsten
Unternehmungen allein taugten.

The question raised is that of man's position in a world where
his worth has come to be reckoned by the work he does. Arnim's
beggars and Eichendorff's Taugenichts are figures demanding
to be considered for what they are, not for what they do. '

3. Narrative Tone

'You don't know about me, without you have read a book by
the name of *The Adventures of Sawyer,* but that ain't no matter.'
Nor do we know anything of the youth sitting on the doorstep
of his father's mill and wiping the sleep out of his eyes – at
least all we know is that he is still alive to tell the tale.

Narration in the first person has its dangers, among them the
'terrible fluidity' that Henry James feared, but in two forms of
the novel these count for little. One is the novel of adventure,
the *Schelmenroman,* the picaresque form of Grimmelshausen's
Simplicissimus, Smollett's *Roderick Random,* or Le Sage's *Gil
Blas*; the other is the comic fantasy of Sterne's *Tristram Shandy,*
or Jean Paul's *Flegeljahre.* In a work such as the *Taugenichts,*
with its picaresque and comic elements, the choice of the hero,
half wanderer, half fool, as his own narrator is therefore natural
enough. Eichendorff, it may be noted, uses this form nowhere
else, with the minor exception of the interpolated 'Geschichte des
Einsiedlers' in *Eine Meerfahrt.* It is this choice of narrator that
very largely sets the *Novelle's* narrative tone or 'resonance',
the element that fuses subject matter, plot, character, symbol,
simile and the rest into one unified effect.

The advantages of relative formlessness and of comic incon-
gruity may be the chief justification for the use of the first-
person narrator in the instances mentioned above, but the
function most commonly attributed to the form is that of
authenticating the events described and giving them a sense of
immediacy (examples of this are the opening paragraphs of
Stifter's *Der Nachsommer,* Gotthelf's *Bauernspiegel,* or the second

version of Keller's *Der grüne Heinrich*). In the *Taugenichts* there is undoubtedly a strong air of unreality and fantasy, but the feeling that this is not just a *Märchen* receives powerful confirmation from the fact that the main participant is notionally addressing us, shadowy though his outlines may be. In the severe third-person narration of Kafka's *Das Schloss* existence itself waits terrifyingly and vainly to be authenticated; but here it is only the quality of the Taugenichts' reverie that is called in question. The reader feels, that is to say, that the melodramatic, or coincidental, or somnambulistic effects spring from the hero's uncertain grasp of his thoughts and story, rather than from any intrinsic inconsistency or unreality of event.

Feise (1936/1950) insists that we have in *Aus dem Leben eines Taugenichts* a boldly exaggerated romantic irony in the fact that the reader guesses at complications of which the narrator himself is apparently ignorant, though in fact he must have known of them, and of the whole outcome, before he could tell the story. But, in practice, the reader suspends disbelief and does not enquire as nicely as this. The Taugenichts' revelations are naive and unsystematic and his understanding, though lively, is limited; these are the factors that condition the reader to accept what he says with a pinch of salt but without pressing him too closely.

Eichendorff's mild irony is achieved by implication. The deeply ironical attitude of Mann towards Hans Castorp involves the intervention of an external controlling narrator, whose view of truth is the norm against which the hero is measured. In the *Taugenichts* event is the norm. The hero is not explicitly measured against given standards of education or conduct or ambition, and indeed it would be difficult even for his later self to make the comparison. The joke, anyway, is not that the Taugenichts' view of truth is inadequate – against all probability his expectations turn out to be justified – but that his understanding of the mechanism of event is deficient. The irony is implicit in his self-confidence; thus it is not the whole of his being that is called in question, but merely one aspect of his personality.

We spoke of the 'later self'. Any first-person narrator's position in time is normally later than the events he describes, in the *Taugenichts* a good deal later. It is, however, only in the first few pages that this is made explicit:

> Es waren noch mehr sehr hübsche, gutgesetzte, nützliche Lehren, ich habe nur seitdem fast alles wieder vergessen.

and

> ach, das alles ist schon lange her!

(There is also in this second quotation some, false, anticipation of the future in the implication that, at the time of writing, the narrator no longer has access to the songs the 'schöne Dame' sang.) The Taugenichts in theory, then, looks back at a previous stage of the self; but any effect this might be expected to have is quite cancelled out by the blank impossibility of envisaging a middle-aged Taugenichts. The actual chronologically older narrator remains wholly notional and the reader is drawn into the stream of events (such as they are), frequently by the use of the historic present:

> Indem, wie ich mich so umsehe, kömmt ein köstlicher Reisewagen ganz nahe an mich heran, der mochte wohl schon einige Zeit hinter mir drein gefahren sein, ohne dass ich es merkte, weil mein Herz so voller Klang war... (Chapter One)
>
> Zuerst, wie ich mich in der weiten, kühlen Vorhalle umschaue, klopft mir jemand mit dem Stocke auf die Schulter. Ich kehre mich schnell um, da steht ein grosser Herr in Staatskleidern... der mich fragt, was ich hier will. Ich war ganz verblüfft... (Chapter One)
>
> Wie ich noch eben so esse und meditiere, wutscht [1826–56 wuscht, 1864 ff. huscht] ein Männlein, das bis jetzt in einer dunklen Ecke der Stube bei seinem Glase Wein gesessen hatte, auf einmal aus seinem Winkel wie eine Spinne auf mich los. (Chapter Four)
>
> Aber wie ich das Glas so auf einmal ausstürzte, bricht sie plötzlich in ein verhaltenes Kichern aus, wird über und über rot, geht in die Tafelstube und macht die Tür hinter sich zu. Was ist da zu lachen? dachte ich ganz verwundert, ich glaube, die Leute in Italien sind alle verrückt. (Chapter Five)

There is, too, a relative suspension of the temporal throughout the *Novelle*. This is achieved by an almost complete absence of detailed points of reference – dates, customs, inventions, wars, reigns – in the story, and by the extreme vagueness of the Taugenichts' denotation of distance and chronology: 'als ich schon eine weite Strecke gegangen war' (end of Chapter Two) is usually about the best he can do. How long is his stay in the Italian castle? or in Rome? And when in the last pages Aurelie, who apparently left Rome 'vergangenen Sommer', says to him:

> Weisst du noch wie du mich damals auf dem Balkone zum letzten-mal sahst? Das war gerade wie heute, auch so ein stiller Abend und Musik im Garten...

we have very little idea of the lapse of time since that 'damals' (repeated three times in the conversation); but despite, or rather because of this, we certainly do not experience it as being at two removes. 'Damals' and 'heute' are not two dates which the reader or the narrator experience as related points in the past, for the standpoint is located in the 'heute' itself.

The reader, that is to say, experiences through the eyes not of the Taugenichts narrator but of the Taugenichts actor – and the air of reverie ensures that the narrator himself also appears to merge with the actor. Thus, says Wiese (1956), since we are not primarily interested in the events or the characters we allow ourselves to look at the world through the moods of the Taugennichts and to succumb to the atmosphere.

Not much is gained by making an elaborate list of the Taugenichts' personal characteristics (as in F. Schnass, *Die Einzelschrift im Deutschunterricht*, vol. II, Bad Heilbrunn, 1955, or Stecher, 1955), calling them all 'romantic' and explaining the narrative in terms of them. It is not the components of his character that concern us but the alternating rhythm of his positive and negative moods. Indeed it is in this very feature that his most engaging traits are found – his naive resiliency and unreflecting optimism. Even the scaffolding of the *Novelle*, the division into chapters, is largely dependent on this rhythm. The *Novelle* is a continuum, each chapter taking up the story of the Taugenichts' pere-grinations where the last one left off; there are no sudden switches of scene or character, there is no alternation of a panoramic description with an isolated episode. But between nearly every chapter some change of mood has taken place, either specifically (as when Chapter Five ends 'bis ich voller Vergnügen einschlief' and Six opens with the recollection, of the dream of the old witch) or, more often, by implication. Most chapters, that is to say, close with the Taugenichts in a state of emotional tension ('ich warf mich in das Gras hin und weinte bitterlich', One; 'mir war gar seltsam zumute, so traurig und doch auch wieder so überaus fröhlich', near the end of Two; 'mir war so kühl und fröhlich zumute', Three; 'so ging's mit mir fort in die weite Welt hinein', Four; 'ich befahl meine Seele dem lieben Gott ... und lief atemlos weiter in das Tal und die Nacht hinaus', Six; 'Sie ist's, sie ist's!' rief ich endlich', Seven; 'mir aber war unterdes alle Lust und Freude in den Brunnen gefallen', Eight; 'ich aber jauchzte am allervergnügtesten', Nine); and then, a breath taken, the next chapter begins on a note of greater sobriety, if not in an entirely different mood.

Eichendorff's chief method of conveying mood in simple to the point of being primitive. He has the Taugenichts explain his emotions:

> Mir war zum Sterben bange. (Chapter One)
> Es war mir schauerlich und seltsam zumute... (Chapter Two)
> die Blumen liess ich ruhig stehen und wachsen, bis der Wind die Blätter verwehte. War mir's doch ebenso wild und bunt verstört im Herzen. (Chapter Two)

or, at the opposite pole:

> Da wurde mir auf einmal ganz klar im Herzen bei dem Morgengrusse, und alle Furcht war vorüber. (Chapter Three)
> Mir war so kühl und fröhlich zumute, als sollt' ich von dem Berge in die prächtige Gegend hinausfliegen. (End of Chapter Three)
> Mir aber war es so sternklar im Herzen, wie damals an dem glückseligen Sonnabend, als ich am offenen Fenster vor der Weinflasche bis tief in die Nacht hinein auf der Geige spielte. (Chapter Eight)

A degree of complication is, however, already evident: both moods tend to be expressed in association with certain features in the natural world. These are more sophisticated than might at first appear and will be discussed later. But it is also true that negative moods frequently find their expression in images of alienation from the world of nature or humanity:

> Jeder hat sein Plätzchen auf der Erde ausgesteckt, hat seinen warmen Ofen, seine Tasse Kaffee, seine Frau, sein Glas Wein zu Abend... – Mir ist's nirgends recht. Es ist, als wäre ich überall eben zu spät gekommen, als hätte die ganze Welt gar nicht auf mich gerechnet. (Chapter Two)
> ... und allen ist's gleich, ob ich noch da bin oder in der Fremde oder gestorben. – Da kam mir die Welt auf einmal so entsetzlich weit und gross vor und ich so ganz allein darin, dass ich aus Herzensgrunde hätte weinen mögen. (Chapter Three)

(Note in both instances the pause for breath before the final, desolate cry, which is thereby made more emphatic.) In the following extract the sense of alienation is achieved by association with two creatures which themselves have very tenuous connexions with the everyday world, the primarily nocturnal hedgehog and owl:

> Ich wickelte mich, gleich einem Igel, in die Stacheln meiner eigenen Gedanken zusammen: vom Schlosse schallte die Tanzmusik nur noch seltener herüber, die Wolken wanderten einsam über den dunkeln Garten weg. Und so sass ich auf dem Baume droben wie die Nachteule, in den Ruinen meines Glückes die ganze Nacht hindurch. (Chapter Two)

(Note the occurrence of 'einsam', even though transferred to the clouds.)

These are the moods through which Wiese asserts that we look at the world of the *Taugenichts*, and it is true that Eichendorff presents their alternation as an important element in the *Novelle*. Yet no one, surely, is very deeply impressed by the Taugenichts' loneliness, unhappiness or despair. (The residual effect of the motifs is another matter altogether.) The alternation of moods, as we have already suggested, does no more than heighten his general joyous acceptance of life and its gifts. He is only very dimly aware of the tragic or daemonic elements in man and nature (perhaps slightly in the journey to the Italian castle, in the approach to Rome, and in the midday heat of the town); there is no need to admonish him, 'Du aber hüte dich, das wilde Tier zu wecken in der Brust, dass es nicht plötzlich ausbricht und dich selbst zerreisst' *(Das Schloss Dürande)*. This is not to deny the existence of these elements in the *Taugenichts;* what has happened is that the choice of the first-person narrator has made it necessary to convey them by indirection.

The truth is that the Taugenichts' moods and reactions are too superficial to be arresting, especially when they are just baldly stated. This is why the whole *Novelle* can seem unbearably trivial on hasty reading. Yet underneath the flickering of event and mood there is a constant current, a paradisal optimism deriving from the attitudes of the hero himself.

His basic reason for accepting the world unsuspiciously is the knowledge that it is ordered by God and that his place in it is assured:

> Den lieben Gott lass ich nur walten;
> Der Bächlein, Lerchen, Wald und Feld
> Und Erd' und Himmel will erhalten,
> Hat auch mein' Sach' aufs best bestellt!

a stanza repeated at the decisive point where he sets off for Italy and reinforced by the porter's description of that country as 'ein schönes Land, da sorgt der liebe Gott für alles.' Schwarz (1957) makes much of the contradictions between this and the poem 'Wer in die Fremde will reisen'. These contradictions, he finds, illustrate 'die wahrhaft unheimliche Doppeldeutigkeit' of the *Novelle;* but he fails to observe that the latter is not the Taugenichts' own song at all: 'Mir fiel dabei auf einmal ein altes Lied recht aufs Herz, das ich noch zu Hause auf meines Vaters Mühle von einem wandernden Handwerksburschen gelernt hatte.'

His self-confidence derives from this identification of himself with God's order: 'Er spielt recht schön', says the village girl, 'Ja' the Taugenichts replies 'das ist eine Gabe Gottes'. At any moment of doubt he has only to remind himself of providential overruling and cast himself upon it. When he loses his way in the mountains after fleeing from the church-going peasant he is undismayed:

> Ich befahl mich daher Gottes Führung, zog meine Violine hervor und spielte alle meine liebsten Stücke durch, dass es recht fröhlich in dem einsamen Walde erklang. (Chapter Three)

After the unnerving coach journey in the wild night-landscape he sees the castle silhouetted on a hilltop and:

> 'Nun Gott befohlen!' rief ich aus und war innerlich ganz munter geworden vor Erwartung... (Chapter Five)

Thus it is appropriate for him to say in almost the same breath in the opening pages of the story:

> 'Nun... wenn ich ein Taugenichts bin, so ist's gut, so will ich in die Welt gehen und mein Glück machen.'

and:

> Mir war es wie ein ewiger Sonntag im Gemüte.

The sense of a perpetual Sunday (with the additional twist of its being a day of rest) and the certainty of finding fortune in the world are aspects of the same trust in God. Sunday afternoons on the grass by the mill are connected at the beginning of Chapter Seven with dreams of Rome' mit... goldenen Toren und hohen, glänzenden Türmen, von denen Engel in goldenen Gewändern sangen.' The providential meeting with the German painter when he is lost in Rome in expressed in similar terms:

> Mir aber, da ich so unverhofft deutsch sprechen hörte, war es nicht anders im Herzen, als wenn die Glocke aus meinem Dorfe am stillen Sonntagsmorgen plötzlich zu mir herüberklänge. 'Gott willkommen, bester Herr Landsmann!' rief ich aus... (Chapter Seven)

Eichendorff's comment on Brentano (*Poetische Literatur*, II, 123), though occasioned by very different works, is almost equally applicable to the *Taugenichts*:

> ... alle diese, an sich heidnischen und untereinander feindlichen Kräfte sind zu heiterer, harmloser Schönheit bewältigt durch eine gewaltigere Kraft, durch eben jenes religiöse Grundgefühl, das nirgend sich wortreich aufdrängend, wie der unsichtbare Hauch eines Sonntagsmorgens

> das Ganze durchweht und von einem Unterschiede zwischen dem
> Diesseits und Jenseits nicht mehr weiss...

It is on this level of 'heitere, harmlose Schönheit' that the
Taugenichts' adventures take place. The misunderstandings, the
coincidences, the countless ridiculous situations, even the fears
and despairs are all poeticized, idealized. Tripped up by his
dressing-gown or by a flower-bed, breaking the spell in the
garden by sneezing a fly off his nose, tumbling from the roof in
his escape from the Italian castle, arguing with the parrot, the
Taugenichts is a figure of fun but at the same time a figure of
innocence, 'der reine Tor'. We may compare Grimmelshausen's
Simplicius in his early days:

> Damals war bei mir nichts Schätzbarliches als ein reines Gewissen
> und aufrichtig frommes Gemüt zu finden, welches mit der edlen
> Unschuld und Einfalt begleitet und umgeben war... (Beginning of
> Chapter Twenty-Four of *Simplicissimus*)

Compared with Grimmelshausen, however, Eichendorff's
comic invention is mediocre; the farcical situations are repe-
titively physical, the jokes at their best a bit thin:

> 'Wer ist da?' rief es auf einmal dicht hinter mir.
> 'Niemand!' schrie ich aus Leibeskräften vor Schreck... (Chapter
> Three)
> 'Parlez-vous français?' sagte ich endlich in meiner Angst zu ihm.
> Er schüttelte mit dem grossen Kopfe, und das war mir sehr lieb,
> denn ich konnte ja auch nicht Französisch. (Chapter Four)

Aus dem Leben eines Taugenichts evokes not a riot of laughter but
a warm glow of pleasure, chiefly concentrated in the hero, his
self-satisfaction and boastings balanced by the wry honesty of
his narration:

> Ich rief den armen Leuten nach allen Seiten recht stolz und zufrieden
> Adjes zu, aber es kümmerte sich eben keiner sehr darum. (Chapter
> One)

The Taugenichts' presentation of the world and of himself is such
that there is created a narrative tone that persuades the reader to
accept the picture of a providential world where innocence is
enough. Within this picture the symbolic values of the separate

elements (nature, wandering, Italy etc.) can seem to operate almost independently. What is pure Eichendorff in the *Taugenichts* as often as not lies in them.

The simplicity and purity of the narrative tone mediated through the Taugenichts is then a religious one. Sophistication is suspect not because of any primitivistic ideal (indeed Gould, it will be remembered, has argued that the *Novelle* is a satire on primitivism) but because it conflicts with a religious experience of wholeness. The argument in *Über naive und sentimentalische Dichtung* could do duty for a Catholic conception of the universe as well as for a Greek one, and paradisal and Rousseauistic states are easily confused. Art itself is in some respects a questionable activity for Eichendorff since it involves a distortion of the personality, and he later quotes with approval Brentano's comparison of a poet with a Strassburg goose, 'der man auf Unkosten von Hirn, Magen u.s.w. die Leber monströs überfüttere; so viele geschmackvolle Liebhaber sie dann auch finden möge, es bleibe doch nur eine kranke Gans' *(Der deutsche Roman*, pp. 203-4).

Romantic sophistication, the predominance of art over religion (and thus over life) he finds particularly in Tieck (cf. his strictures on *Sternbald* in *Der deutsche Roman*, p. 217), whose delicate irony lets us sense quite clearly that the author himself does not really believe in the things about which he is writing (*Poetische Literatur*, II, 71). This irony, Tieck believes, is the sign of true inspiration, it is the

> Aethergeist, der, so sehr er das Werk bis in seine Tiefen hinab mit Liebe durchdrang, doch befriedigt und unbefangen über dem Ganzen schwebt und es von dieser Höhe nur (so wie der Geniessende), erschaffen und fassen kann.

Eichendorff replies:

> Diese Auffassung ist allerdings... vollkommen richtig in Bezug auf das Verhältniss des Dichters zu der formellen Behandlung eines Kunstwerks [cf. the lightly ironical way in which Leonhard is allowed to criticize the formal action of novels and, by implication, of this *Novelle* – Chapter Ten]; nicht aber wo der Inhalt oder Geist der

Dichtung ein christlicher sein soll, in seinem Verhältnisse zum
Christentum, das eben kein blosses Kunstwerk ist; hier ist der Dichter
kein Erschaffender, kein Geniessender, sondern ein Empfangender,
ein Glaubender. Die Religion... ist vielmehr selbst jener Aether-
geist...

This is the spirit that hovers over *Aus dem Leben eines Taugenichts*.

4. *Thematic Monotone*

Everybody said it was a real beautiful oath, and asked Tom if
he got it out of his own head. He said, some of it, but the
rest was out of... books.

We have seen that the ethos of the *Taugenichts* is a function of
the first-person narrator; but in the total aesthetic impact of
the *Novelle* a complex web of motif and symbol also plays its
part. Eichendorff's overt intention emerges through the narrative tone, but his poetic personality asserts itself thematically
enciphered.

The themes are not, at first sight, in any way remarkable; they
seem to be the commonplaces of romanticism, and indeed that is
often what they are. There are relatively few of them and they
keep turning up in all Eichendorff's works. His lyrics, in particular, seem littered with moribund motifs. There is, perhaps, a
general justification for the use of formalized expressions,
stereotyped stylistic forms and recurring motifs in the Romantic
movement. They are, Kohlschmidt (1950/55) suggests, a counter-
poise to subjectivism, an anchor in the traditional and stable.
The formalizing tendency, easily though it degenerated into
mannerism in Biedermeier almanachs, must therefore not be
reduced to mere poverty of expressive invention. Even if this
appears to be the explanation in Eichendorff or Wackenroder,
it is clearly not true of Tieck, Novalis or Brentano. And may
it not be (Rehder, 1957) that what we have even in Eichendorff's
case is a virtuosity in using the only possible symbolic forms for
the presentation of certain fundamental states?

Yet Eichendorff's limitations in the narrative genre are plain to see, however irrelevant one may judge them to be in individual works. He is unable to give outlines to character, he has little narrative drive (though more than many of his Romantic contemporaries), his powers of concrete description are meagre, his social and emotional range is a restricted one, he suffers to some degree from a poverty of linguistic expression. Some of these weaknesses are more apparent than real – his descriptions are rich in atmospheric power, his language is strongly emotive even if stereotyped – but it is difficult to deny that others of the limitations are dictated more by inadequacy than by inclination. Rehder, for instance, illustrates how his imagery is completely conditioned by his aristocratic background. The situations in which he sets his characters are mainly aristocratic (even in the *Taugenichts*), removed from everyday existence and from such fundamental human experiences as suffering, guilt and death. One may recall Lukács' judgement: 'Wir haben es also offenbar mit dem reinsten Typus des feudalen Romantikers zu tun.'

His diction, then, is stereotyped and, in a sense, monotonous. Jahn has shown (1937, pp. 76–7) how his reading of Tieck between 1804 and 1806 gave at first a Romantic colouring to his vocabulary, but since Tieck's language was itself limited by his preference for generalities the result was still what she calls 'eine ganz erstaunliche Einförmigkeit der Sprache' (p. 97). This reveals itself in the lack of particularity in the substantives (e.g. only very rarely is 'Baum' more closely defined as 'Eiche', 'Linde' etc.) and the recurrence of simple epithets. Of some 1,700 instances of the use of attributive adjectives in the *Taugenichts*, 400 are confined to nine simple epithets (lang, 58 times; gross, 86; klein, 39; hoch, 26; hell, 15; dunkel, 15; schön, 103; prächtig, 24; still, 40).[1] It seems probable that Eichendorff did not consciously will this uniformity of vocabulary but, on the other hand, it is arguable that the resultant simplicity gives

[1] Dr. B. A. Rowley points out that these are not Tieck's preferred epithets (e.g. 'süss' is missing), and that they have more in common with those of Mörike. This is only one of the many valuable suggestions for which I am indebted to him.

an air of primitive freshness to the whole. Jahn, in connexion with this and with the simplicity of sentence structure (cf. the way the *Taugenichts* opens with a series of more or less interchangeable main clauses), speaks of the atmosphere of the *Märchen*, and one might even catch an echo of the *epitheton ornans*. Indeed, although the influence of the first generation of Romantic writers on much of Eichendorff's style is undisputed (as one more example one might mention his compound nouns), there are other occasions when we catch an echo of *Hermann und Dorothea*, or of Voss's *Luise* or his translation of Homer. And at other times we look forward to earthier writers (compare some of the exaggerated similes with those of Gotthelf), or to the more genteel and pallid language of the minor Biedermeier writers.

But it is not only the range of linguistic expression that is limited. We have already indicated how derivative and stereotyped many of the themes and motifs themselves are. Eichendorff was well aware of this, as witness the passage in *Viel Lärmen um Nichts* (1833) where he satirizes his own use of the guitar motif – which was probably derived from Dorothea Schlegel's *Florentin* (1801):

'Mein Gott!' rief er, 'Graf Leontin aus *Ahnung und Gegenwart!*' – 'Ist gleich an der Guitarre zu erkennen', fiel ihm der Dicke ins Wort; 'er kann nicht wohl gespeist zu haben sagen, ohne einen Griff in die Saiten dazu.'

Because the themes were the common property of the reading public of the day, they could, however, be adapted and elaborated into something as new as Tom's oath. Eichendorff was able to use their associative power – and he frequently did this somewhat mechanically – but he was also able to achieve new contextual associations. Motifs in his work depend a good deal on the context for their shade of meaning and his peculiar achievement lies in the way he organizes them into symbolic patterns. Thus though the wood, the valleys, the moon or the night are used as romantic motifs, they come together to present a symbolic picture of the natural order, and a slight rearrangement of them can often change the meaning entirely.

Eichendorff criticism has too generally seemed to insist that all the motifs are symbols or that they are all stereotypes. The problem is more complicated. It is that of distinguishing between the atmospheric motifs and structural or linguistic formulas, deriving mainly from his reading and personal experiences and used fairly casually, and those more profound symbolic rhythms, similar perhaps in derivation, that carry the meaning of the *Novelle*. Any such distinction will at times be forced and blurred at the edges, but even the attempt to make it may help to show the surprisingly successful way in which Eichendorff puts new wine into old bottles.

It will be convenient to consider first some of the main structural motifs and general themes that are obviously derivative and apparently stereotyped, in order to see what new use Eichendorff makes of them; and to reserve for the next chapter the more consistently coherent and purposeful use of motifs from the natural world.

The lyrics.

A typical structural motif in the fiction of the Romantic movement is the interpolated lyric (P. Neuburger, *Die Verseinlage in der Prosadichtung der Romantik*, Leipzig, 1924 = Palaestra 145). In general, Eichendorff's lyrics stand isolated in their context, with very little psychological motivation for their occurrence; there is perhaps slightly more in the *Taugenichts* in that the hero often sings for some particular purpose, but this is a marginal distinction. Their purpose, here as elsewhere, is to epitomize the mood and to achieve a concentration of meaning and experience. Their success in doing this depends on Eichendorff's superiority as a lyricist to such models as Tieck and Arnim.

Lyric interpolations occur fourteen times in the *Taugenichts* and, of these, three are repetitions: the last stanza of 'Wem Gott will rechte Gunst erweisen' (*Der frohe Wandersmann*), the first of 'Wohin ich geh' und schaue' (*Der Gärtner*), and 'Schweigt der

Menschen laute Lust' *(Der Abend).*[1] Small discrepancies appear
between the versions of the first two; that in *Der frohe Wandersmann* need not detain us since the variant 'tut erhalten' for
'will erhalten' is foreshadowed by the existence of both in the
MS discussed earlier. The second represents a change of attitude
that is of some interest: 'Vom Berg ins Himmelsblaue' becomes
'Vom Berg hinab in die Aue', Eichendorff's more customary
viewpoint. The change is scarcely motivated by the context
and trifling though it is suggests something of the rapid alternation of mood in the *Taugenichts* (in this case a slightly more
realistic, down-to-earth note is produced by the new version).

In many instances the lyrics are reminiscent of the *Singspiel,*
the halfway house between opera and comedy, with its spoken
dialogue interspersed with songs and its words and music having a simple, direct appeal. This is especially true of the Taugenichts' minor snatches, 'Wenn der Hoppevogel schreit', 'Wenn
ich ein Vöglein wär,' of Guido's 'Darum bin ich dir gewogen',
of the chorus of little girls singing 'Wir bringen dir den Jung-
fernkranz', or of the male trio of the Prague students. They all
contribute to the light-hearted, slightly unreal effect but are
otherwise unremarkable and almost interchangeable with those
in many other Romantic *Novellen.*

The 'arias' themselves are a different matter. The four major
ones sung by the Taugenichts himself, *Der frohe Wandersmann,*
Der Gärtner, Heimweh ('Wer in die Fremde will wandern')
and *An der Grenze* ('Die treuen Berg' stehn auf der Wacht'),
come at strategic points in the narrative. (Bauer's article, 1933,
is of little interest on these or the other songs; he even attributes
one of Guido's songs to the Taugenichts.)

The first lyric, as we have already seen, sets the basic tone for
the *Novelle* as a whole – man should commit himself to careless
wandering rather than to utilitarian drudgery and God's providential order will embrace him as it does the natural world.

---

[1] The titles are those in the *Gedichte,* Berlin, 1837, except for the
'Prager Studenten', not included among the poems until *Werke,* 1841.

The echoes of Georg Neumark's *Trostlied* (1640/41) do no more than confirm this:

> Wer nur den lieben Gott lässt walten
> Und hoffet auf ihn allezeit,
> Der wird ihn wunderlich erhalten
> In aller Not und Traurigkeit.
>
> . . .
>
> Was helfen uns die schwere Sorgen?
> Was hilft uns unser Weh und Ach?
> Was hilft es, dass wir alle Morgen
> Beseufzen unser Ungemach?
>
> . . .

Der Gärtner concentrates the Taugenichts' love experience in its early stages and points also his apparent isolation; this, unusually, is made clear contextually by the use of the pedant in the boating party to emphasize the gap between polite society and the untutored, natural boy. Still, the isolation is more apparent than real, for despite the fact that there are tears in his eyes even as he sings ('das Herz wollte mir zerspringen von dem Liede vor Scham und vor Schmerz, es fiel mir jetzt auf einmal alles recht ein, wie *sie* so schön ist und ich so arm und verspottet und verlassen von der Welt') the 'schöne Frau' has not associated herself with the teasing but has kept her eyes lowered all through the song.

We have already noted that *Heimweh* is not strictly the Taugenichts' own song; it is one he had learnt from a wandering journeyman when he was at home at the mill. Its origin is not accidental: it strengthens the evocation of home whilst suggesting that some are homeless. In circumstances so strange that the Taugenichts is in danger of losing his very identity, the song provides the stabilizing influences of family and love.

An der Grenze is structurally the most remarkable of the four. The Taugenichts has turned his back on the confusions of the foreign land, and the first chapter of his return opens with this song. Beginning a chapter with a lyric is a device often adopted by Eichendorff in order to set the tone for the whole section, and

here we find the Taugenichts not yet wholly out of danger:
'Wer streicht bei stiller Morgenzeit / Da aus der Fremde durch
die Heid?' (we shall discuss later the play on the word 'Heide').
But the natural world of his homeland is more friendly than this
('Nun grüssen Bach und Vöglein zart / Und Wälder rings nach
Landesart') and the church also beckons him home ('Der
Stephansturm auch ganz von fern / Guckt übern Berg und säh
mich gern'). The Taugenichts is on the frontier between his
two dreams, wandering and home, not merely that between two
countries.

One other lyric must be mentioned: Guido's evening song (the
morning one is typical enough but is only a part of an earlier
version). This comes immediately after the Taugenichts' talk
with the hunchback, the nearest thing the tale has to a representative of evil and of the daemonic forces ('manchmal kam es
mir vor, als schlüpfte eine lange dunkle Gestalt hinter den Hasel-
nussträuchern vor dem Hause vorüber und guckte durch die
Zweige' – a typical representation of the devil). The sense of
unease inspired by him is heightened by Guido's song: 'Und es
schweifen leise Schauer / Wetterleuchtend durch die Brust.'
Nature is not all it seems to be by day; it is charged with history:

> Rauscht die Erde wie in Träumen
> Wunderbar mit allen Bäumen,
> Was dem Herzen kaum bewusst,
> Alte Zeiten, linde Trauer...

History, the past, stands still and is preserved in ruins, moonlit
gardens, under a cover of grass, flowers or ivy. 'Der Vergangenheit wird verewigt durch Verzauberung, Erstarrung, Versinken
in Schlaf und Natur' (Emrich, 1939). For a moment the action
of the *Novelle* is suspended, lost in a dreamlike state, swallowed
up by the animal and vegetable life of this strange country, of
which the Taugenichts has just said:

> Denn mir war in dem fremden Lande nicht anders, als wäre ich mit
> meiner deutschen Zunge tausend Klafter tief ins Meer versenkt, und
> allerlei unbekanntes Gewürm ringelte sich und rauschte da in der
> Einsamkeit um mich her und glotzte und schnappte nach mir.

And when he awakes in the morning he finds that the 'painters' have fled and that he is alone indeed, caught up by the hostility of things.

Mechanical and artificial though the use of interpolated lyrics often is in Romantic fiction, Eichendorff's not excluded, it is clear that in the *Taugenichts* he has given some of them a structural function, either that of preparing or concentrating a mood or that of summoning up airy scenic pictures.

Dreams.

Another type of inset is the dream. The imprecision and imaginative scope made possible by the dream state proved as attractive to Eichendorff as to other Romantic writers (see also I. Weidekampf, *Traum und Wirklichkeit in der Romantik*, Leipzig, 1932 = Palaestra 182). A typical locution in the *Taugenichts* is 'so dass ich nicht recht wusste, ob ich träumte oder wachte', and the association of the dream state with confusion is very marked:

> Mir verwirrten sich ordentlich die Gedanken, als läge ich in einem Traum und könnte gar nicht aufwachen. (Chapter Three)

This is very reminiscent of the opening pages of *Lucinde* and has its parallels too in the way the Taugenichts is frequently described as 'wie betrunken', 'wie bezaubert', 'wie verzaubert'. The paraphernalia of confusion of identity, dressing-up and the rest of it might also be thought to have some affinities to this, though these operatic or romantic conventions must not be taken too seriously (certainly not in *Die Freier*).

The content of the Taugenichts' Roman dreams is nostalgic (his village and the mill), sensuous ('ein warmer Sommerregen sprühte und glänzte in der Sonne', 'mir träumte... von schönen, dunkelgrünen, einsamen Gründen, wo Quellen rauschten und Bächlein gingen und bunte Vögel wunderbar sangen'), infinitely distant ('mir träumte von himmelblauen Blumen'). The elements are similar in both of them and it might be said that this is a handy way of introducing at this stage these various moods that are not completely revealed in waking life.

But the first extended dream the Taugenichts has, in the orchard as he sets off for Italy, is more complex. People are going to church and over the fields the sound of the bells comes to the Taugenichts who, as he falls asleep, is thinking of the mill and of the garden of his 'schöne, gnädige Frau' – 'und wie das alles nun so weit, weit lag.' (It is typical of the atmospheric rather than literal accuracy of the *Novelle* that it is still only the morning of his departure from the castle, so he cannot be unduly far away). The dream proper begins with his beloved's appearance from the landscape round about him, hovering in the air with long white veils trailing in the dawn. This might initially be taken to convey innocence – the figures of saints or first communion – and the dawn of hope. The scene of the dream then changes to the mill, where all is quiet and deserted, as though everyone is at church. There is now a hint of danger and isolation in the fact that it is indeed Sunday but the Taugenichts is out alone in the world. The 'schöne, gnädige Frau' is well-disposed towards him and as she takes him by the hand and sings to him she appears to be a kind of guardian angel. When her face is seen in the pool, however, it is 'noch vieltausendmal schöner, aber mit sonderbaren grossen Augen, die mich so starr ansahen, dass ich mich beinahe gefürchtet hätte', and something wild or supernatural has evidently invaded the dream. Then the wind rises, the sails of the mill turn faster, the pool darkens and the water is ruffled, the face turns pale, the veils 'flatterten entsetzlich in langen Spitzen wie Nebelstreifen hoch am Himmel empor', the noise increases as if the porter were blowing his bassoon, and with his heart beating violently the Taugenichts awakes. In these last elements the dream's approach to nightmare hinges first of all on the way daemonic powers are suggested in the movements of the natural world – wind, light, water, sound. The beloved retains a link with the heavens (the veils 'flatterten... hoch am Himmel empor') but the temporal, in its most threatening forms, now touches her too (her face pales, the veils flap 'entsetzlich' and 'wie Nebelstreifen' – an echo of Goethe's *Erlkönig*). She has momentarily become the Venus

figure of the *Marmorbild;* the pool is the same, the paleness of
face, the eyes, the reflection in the water, the wind, the veil.
Even the vocabulary is repeated:

So in Gedanken schritt [Florio] noch lange fort, als er unerwartet
bei einem grossen, von hohen Bäumen rings umgebenen Weiher
anlangte. Der Mond, der eben über die Wipfel trat, beleuchtete
scharf ein marmornes Venusbild, das dort dicht am Ufer auf einem
Steine stand, als wäre die Göttin soeben erst aus den Wellen aufge-
taucht und betrachte nun, selber verzaubert, das Bild der eigenen
Schönheit... Als er wieder aufblickte, schien auf einmal alles wie
verwandelt... Ein stärkerer Wind kräuselte den Weiher in trübe
Wellen, das Venusbild, so fürchterlich weiss und regungslos, sah ihn
fast schreckhaft mit den steinernen Augenhöhlen aus der grenzen-
losen Stille an. Ein nie gefühltes Grausen überfiel da den Jüngling.

Or later in the same *Novelle:*

> Und unterm duftgen Schleier,
> So oft der Lenz erwacht,
> Webt in geheimer Feier
> Die alte Zaubermacht.

The Taugenichts' dream is a conventional way of associating the
natural and supernatural. The motifs in the dream are also
conventional enough: the romantic associations of 'Weiher'
are sufficiently attested in Grimm's Dictionary, the flowing
veils are a traditional accompaniment of mythological, saintly
or poetic figures (cf. Goethe's *Zueignung*), the fixed gaze of the
magic temptress occurs in *Faust*, Part One, lines 4190-2. But
the total effect in the context is not unoriginal: the Taugenichts,
launching out into the unknown world, feels the cold wind
of evil even on the love that is otherwise his protective shield. The
seas of earth are not all plain sailing, though it is characteristic of
the *Taugenichts* that in the long run the winds blow more gently
here than in Eichendorff's other *Novellen:* 'Es hatte sich wirklich
ein Wind erhoben, der leise über mir durch den Apfelbaum
ging.'

The Dreamer.

Derivative Romantic themes and motifs also reveal themselves in human character or situations; the dreamer himself is a type.

The Taugenichts is, in many ways, a Romantic 'original', deriving in part from the fool of Grimmelshausen and Cervantes, developed by Sterne and Wieland (cf. H. Meyer, *Der Typus des Sonderlings in der deutschen Literatur*, Amsterdam, 1943). The fool is, however, objectively measurable against the norms of morality, order and reason; the original is a product of Romantic subjectivism, of the feeling of strain between the demands of reality and the primacy of the emotional inner life. This sense of strain is what Eichendorff later regards as particularly characteristic of Jean Paul. In Hoffmann the dichotomy becomes more explicitly tragic, but in the *Taugenichts* a happy compromise is achieved by making reality poetic without falling into the vaguely ethereal like the early Romanticists. The Taugenichts is, indeed, a dreamer, but he is not wholly divorced from his surroundings. Lukács is grinding a political axe when he writes: 'Es ist auch kein Zufall, dass der Held... ebenfalls ein Bauernsohn, wenn auch ein etwas märchenhaft stilisierter ist'; the Taugenichts has clearly very little in common with the early 19th-century peasant. But his plebeian origins, though little stressed, do give him a common touch that is emphasized by contrast with other characters. Indeed Eichendorff here manages to have it both ways; he ridicules the idealized picture of the *Volk*, whilst to some extent adopting it himself in his simple and innocent narrator. This can be seen not only in the episode with the foppish young man in the boat but also in the figure of the student who watches the Taugenichts amusing the servants at the Italian castle by playing his fiddle:

> Zuletzt kam auch noch der blasse Student neugierig hervor, warf einige verächtliche Blicke auf das Spektakel und wollte ganz vornehm wieder weitergehen. (Chapter Six)

Another instance is that of the pleasanter, but still comic, conductor in the Hoffmann tableau, who gets up a dance when the Taugenichts takes out his violin:

> 'Bravo, bravissimo, ein deliziöser Einfall!' rief der lustige Kenner von den Künsten und lief sogleich von einem zum andern, um ein

ländliches Divertissement, wie er's nannte, einzurichten. (Chapter Eight)

The Artist.

Möbus has suggested (1960, p. 128) that there is also something Franciscan about the Taugenichts; he justifies this view by reference to a Görres essay of 1826, 'Der hl. Franziskus ein Troubadour'. But it seems more likely that in natural simplicity he has more in common with the artistic innocence of vision in Brentano's *Chronicka eines fahrenden Schülers*, of which a part was published in 1818. Is the Taugenichts then merely the Romantic artist in disguise, Eichendorff's ideal vision of the poet, as Bosselmann-Franzen (1939) argues? Certainly his anti-philistinism is clearly enough expressed; he has a poor opinion of the utilitarian, the vegetable garden or the apple-trees meant for profit rather than for sitting in. He is infuriated by the merely purposive, the porter's criticism of hunting, the young girl's notion that he could make a living by playing his fiddle. And yet he is not wholly free of philistinism himself: the dressing-gown, the slippers, the pipe and parasol present a considerable temptation to him, the porter is almost his favourite character and he ends up in the highly philistine state of getting married to the porter's niece. It might be well, too, to compare the Taugenichts' actions with those of a genuine artist:

> Er zeichnete nun in der frischen Morgenkühle immer fleissig fort, während er ein Liedchen dazu sang und zuweilen durch das offene Fenster in die prächtige Gegend hinausblickte. Ich aber schnitt mir unterdes noch eine Butterstolle... (Chapter Seven)

Still, the Taugenichts is certainly an artist of a kind, one of a long line of wandering minstrels. He is not a Hoffmannesque virtuoso manqué (see G. C. Schoolfield, *The Figure of the Musician in German Literature*, Chapel Hill, 1956), nor a gypsy rogue of the Brentano kind, nor one of Uhland's ballad-singers. He makes music because it pleases him and because it fixes a mood; it is an expression of his own childlike personality. 'Ich sagte ihm, er sollte nur seine Pfennige behalten, ich spielte nur so, aus Freude, weil ich wieder bei Menschen wäre' (Chapter Three). It is when he is being most himself that he plays the fiddle; during the philistine period as toll-keeper it hangs neglected on the wall. It is a feature of his love for Aurelie:

> die hat sich in allen Winkeln von Rom nach... einem jungen Musikanten mit der Geige erkundigen lassen (Chapter Seven)

as the chambermaid mockingly recognizes:

> 'Ach,' unterbrach sie mich, 'die ist ja lange schon wieder in Deutschland, mitsamt deiner tollen Amour. Und da lauf du nur auch wieder hin! Sie schmachtet ohnedies nach dir, da könnt ihr zusammen die Geige spielen und in den Mond gucken...'

Yet there is also a breath of art's transcendental function in one of the Taugenichts' refererences to his fiddle:

> 'Ja,' sagt' ich, 'komm nur her, du getreues Instrument! Unser Reich ist nicht von dieser Welt!'

Too much should not be read into this, but enough has perhaps been said to show that Eichendorff's wandering minstrel is not as wholly stereotyped as we might have remembered. It is in Wilhelm Müller rather than Eichendorff that we get the completely conventional picture.

In other respects, though, Eichendorff's musical instruments are little more than Romantic stage-properties and the minor musicians are stock figures. The musical references in the Taugenichts itself are more numerous than detailed; it is seldom that he goes beyond the most general and formalized indication of the quality of voice or instrumental sound (whether of guitar, bassoon, clarinet or zither): '[Guido] spielte sehr geschickt auf einen Zither... und sang dazu wie eine Nachtigall' (Chapter Four) is typical. In this context Aurelie herself is conventionally depicted: 'Sie nahm auch die Gitarre in den weissen Arm' (Chapter One), but her guitar-playing does in fact acquire the structural importance of a leitmotif in the Novelle, the reaction to the sound of the instrument being the cause of the Taugenichts' flight from the Italian castle into the student's arms and an accompaniment to his confusion in the episode with the counterfeit 'schöne, gnädige Frau' in Rome.

The primary characteristic of music-making in the *Taugenichts* is that it all takes place in the open air and thus tends to become part of the natural scene; this is, of course, especially so with the horn. In human terms the function of music is a subordinate one and certainly does not support any claim for the primacy of art in the hero's life. The wandering minstrel's wandering is more significant than his music, though in relation to the natural world both produce a similar effect of spaciousness, of a desire to extend the bound of sensation or to reach out for eternity.

Wandering.

No motif seems more characteristic of Eichendorff than that of wandering, and despite its lavish presence in Uhland, Müller and the rest it finds its most complete expression in his works. In *Viel Lärmen um Nichts* the office-bound official dreams:

> Da über die Berge, zwischen den ersten Morgenlichtern, sehe ich einen jungen rüstigen Gesellen wandern, einen grünen Eichenzweig auf dem Hut, die braunen Locken vom Tau funkelnd, so frisch und keck, als gings ins Paradies.

This is the idealization of a picture derived from the Florestan of Tieck's *Sternbald*, or from Dorothea Schlegel's *Florentin*, from Brentano, from Goethe's *Meister*, from Cervantes and no doubt many others. The Taugenichts, too, is walking towards paradise, but his wandering has a double edge to it. Is is a joyful plunge into the future ('mich packte da auf einmal wieder meine alte Reiselust: alle die alte Wehmut und Freude und grosse Erwartung' – Chapter Two), but it also contains a threat of isolation. We see this most clearly in the passage where the Taugenichts is listening to the Prague students:

> 'Und wenn dann endlich die Vakanz kommt, und die andern fahren und reiten zu ihren Eltern fort, da wandern wir mit unseren Instrumenten unterm Mantel durch die Gassen zum Tore hinaus, und die ganze Welt steht uns offen.'

Ich weiss nicht – wie er so erzählte – ging es mir recht durchs Herz, dass so gelehrte Leute so ganz verlassen sein sollten auf der Welt. Ich dachte dabei an mich, wie es mir eigentlich selber nicht anders ginge, und die Tränen traten mir in die Augen. (Chapter Nine)

'Die ganze Welt steht uns offen' and 'so ganz verlassen auf der Welt'; this is the perpetual tension in the *Novelle*, the reason for the Taugenichts' constant changes of mood. In wandering man becomes nature, and thus exposed to the perils of the natural order.

Thus the Taugenichts' normal state is not one of complete inactivity; he soon gets tired of the life of complete idleness in the Italian castle. Wandering is a release from everyday bourgeois commitments but it is quite opposed to the spirit of Friedrich Schlegel's 'Idylle über den Müssiggang' in *Lucinde*. Schlegel writes, 'Und also wäre ja das höchste, vollendetste Leben nichts als ein *reines Vegetieren*.' But the vegetative is one of the main dangers the Eichendorff hero has to avoid.

Italy.

The Taugenichts' wanderlust is given direction by the attraction of Italy. 'Pilgrime sind wir alle, die wir Italien suchen', wrote Goethe in the Venetian Epigrams, and it is a commonplace that this dream of the South became an essential ingredient of the German tradition in the course of the late eighteenth and nineteenth centuries (cf. W. Waetzoldt, *Das klassische Land. Wandlungen der Italiensehnsucht*, Leipzig, 1927, and Häusler, 1939, with Hans Castorp's dream in *Der Zauberberg* as its most brilliant evocation in literature). For the Romantics Italy meant a landscape rich in mood, brilliantly coloured yet often desolate, its ruins charged with antiquity and transience together. It was the home of religious art and of the Catholic Church; its people were sensuous, idle, beautiful, natural, careless of time. It is a generalized picture of this kind that underlies Eichendorff's picture of Italy in the *Taugenichts*. Cysarz (*Von Schiller zu Nietzsche*, Halle/Saale, 1928, p. 100) is very severe on his unrealistic presentation: 'Seine Südlandschaften sind sternbaldisierende Märchen- und Wunschbilder mit barockem Kitsch adjustiert', and Ricarda Huch made much the same complaint. Criticism is naturally encouraged by the knowledge that Eichendorff never visited Italy and must have relied entirely on secondhand information.

He seems to owe most of his detailed knowledge to the painter Philipp Veit, to Hermann Friedlaender of Königsberg, who in 1820 published his *Ansichten von Italien während einer Reise in den Jahren 1815/16* (Bianchi, 1937), and to the MS diaries of his intimate friend Carl Albert Eugen Schaeffer (Scheyer, 1956). The picture of the artistic life in Rome derives from the Nazarene circle, and particularly from the Veits, Johannes and Philipp, the sons of Dorothea Schlegel by her first marriage. (The 'Nazarene' group of painters, with its best known representatives Overbeck, Cornelius, Schadow, Schnorr and the Veits, grew up about 1810 at the deserted San Isidoro monastery near Rome. The group wished to return to the style of Raphael and Michelangelo and held that art should serve religious rather than sensuous or aesthetic ends.) It is probable that the unnamed German painter in the *Taugenichts* is modelled on Philipp Veit, and one of the paintings in the studio is identified by Bianchi as being the second version of a portrait of Gräfin Julie Zichy, a friend of the Schlegels and the Veits. Eichendorff may have seen an earlier version in Philipp Veit's studio in Vienna in 1812 (cf. *SW*, XI, 308). Scheyer also mentions W. von Schadow's portrait of Adelheid von Humboldt, painted in Rome in 1817. The other work in the studio, which is in the cartoon state, is of the Virgin and Child with two shepherd boys kneeling by the hut – a likely enough subject for a Nazarene painting.

Eichendorff's Italy is perhaps not very readily distinguishable from his Germany if one thinks merely of the landscape descriptions, though sometimes his lack of direct experience may give his Italian settings a more stagy air. But Italy is for him less a geographical location than an idea, and it is this whole idea that forms the motif. Seidlin goes further when he analyses the

scene in which the Taugenichts approaches Rome (1953/56).
The city, he argues, is not presented visually; it is not what
lies before us but what has long existed in the Taugenichts'
dreams. Time and space are annulled and we lose our orientation
in the real world. This opens the way for what is 'real' in the
proper sense, and a city appears which is the heavenly city, the
city of cities, man's long home. We are then jerked back into
the action but, instead of topographical detail, are given the
boundless sea and the sky, and ambiguous or paradoxical
metaphors. And we are still separated from the city of salvation
by a grey and gloomy heath, where everything is dead and
earthbound, material and unredeemed. Even the narrative style
becomes objective – 'sie sagen' instead of 'ich hatte gehört'.
The ego has withdrawn from the dead world. The pun on
'Heide', too, links geography and theology; it is a metaphysical
landscape with the honest Taugenichts moving through it
towards his salvation. And when the angels sing through the
evening hush, Seidlin continues: 'Sie singen herüber aus dem
Dort und Immer. Und für wen singen sie? Für einen Taugenichts,
der nach Rom kommt? Nein, für einen gläubig-frommen
Menschen, für jeden gläubig-frommen Menschen, der gewan-
dert ist durch die Welt der kalten, unerlösten Wirklichkeit, der
treu geblieben ist dem Märchenbild aus Kindertagen und nun
endlich, endlich vor den Toren steht – zum Paradies.'

Seidlin's article merits this lengthy summary because it indi-
cates the complexities inherent in Eichendorff's use of such
commonplace motifs as Italy and Rome, though it implies too
readily perhaps that the complexities are peculiar to Eichendorff.
In one instance, too, his analysis seems forced. He lays considerable stress on the 'und' of 'eine uralte Stadt und die Frau
Venus'; it is, he says, a meaningless and grotesque connexion
which points to the artificiality of relationships in the merely
material. But, neat though this argument is, it cannot stand.
For there is the closest connexion between the two elements,
one that is made explicit in three stanzas of Fortunato's song in

Das Marmorbild:

> Versunknes Reich zu Füssen,
> Vom Himmel fern und nah
> Aus andrem Reich ein Grüssen –
> Das ist Italia!
>
> . .
>
> Frau Venus hört das Locken,
> Der Vögel heitern Chor,
> Und richtet froh erschrocken
> Aus Blumen sich empor.
>
> Sie sucht die alten Stellen,
> Das luftge Säulenhaus,
> Schaut lächelnd in die Wellen
> Der Frühlingsluft hinaus.

or in Fortunat's song in *Dichter und ihre Gesellen*:

> Es rauschen die Wipfel und schauern,
> Als machten zu dieser Stund
> Um die halbversunkenen Mauern
> Die alten Götter die Rund.

This, as Fortunato's song later shows, is the conflict between Venus and the Virgin, heathen antiquity (the ruins of the city) and Christianity, unredeemed nature and God's world, the daemonic and the divine.

This theme is found in every one of Eichendorff's *Novellen* but it is not peculiar to him. It is Romantic mythology's reaction against the Classical picture of the gods of antiquity; something of it is found in Tieck, something in Arnim, something in Zacharias Werner's poem 'Italien', of which Eichendorff later wrote: 'Bei seinem Eintritt in Rom aber ist es zunächst, als stutzte er innerlichst vor den Schranken der Vergänglichkeit und Ewigkeit, die dort über dem Grabe einer untergegangenen Welt sich mahnend begegnen' *(Poetische Literatur*, II, 110–11). Rome and Italy fit neatly into the symbolic pattern of Eichendorff's works without his having to deform the motifs as he found them. The common dream of Italy is laced with dangers, even the porter after he has spoken of it as 'ein schönes Land, da sorgt der liebe Gott für alles' goes on, though in ignorance, to mention the tarantula. But its paradisal appeal remains to the end of the *Novelle*, for though the Taugenichts has turned his back on it ('Ich nahm mir nun fest vor, den falschen Italien... auf ewig den Rücken zu kehren', Chapter Eight), he has brought back with him a pocketful of almonds which he cracks with Aurelie as he announces that they must return to Italy after their wedding.

These, then, are some of the structural patterns and themes in the *Taugenichts*: the interspersed lyrics, the dreams, the dreamer, the original, the idler, the minstrel, the wanderer, Italy, Rome. They are all the common coin of the period, and Eichendorff appears to have little else to offer. Even the 'realistic' descriptions ('Die Mägde gingen mit zerzottelten Haaren herum und hatten die offenen Halstücher unordentlich um das gelbe Fell hängen', in Chapter Four; or '... ich konnte darin die hellerleuchteten Stuben und allerlei lumpiges Gesindel sehen, das wie dunkle Schatten um das Herdfeuer herumhockte', in Chapter Five) suggest genre paintings as much as direct original observation. Yet we have seen that all these elements do not remain mere conventional counters in his hands. Often, though not always, the context invests them with additional meaning, whilst their very familiarity suggests, for the German at any rate, a traditional, universal application. We know that the scenery consists of old and battered props, but touched up and rearranged they create their own world.

5. *Symbolic Overtones*

The stars was shining, and the leaves rustled in the woods ever so mournful; and I heard an owl, away off, who-whooing about somebody that was dead, and a whippowill and a dog crying about somebody that was going to die; and the wind was trying to whisper something to me and I couldn't make out what it was...

Most of the action of the *Taugenichts* takes place in the open air. We are exposed to the natural world, the hieroglyph of eternity a swell as the vestment of evil. This world speaks to us in its component parts, in the individual landscapes themselves:

> Wie wahr ist es, sagte Friedrich, dass jede Gegend schon von Natur ihre eigentümliche Schönheit, ihre eigene Idee hat, die sich mit ihren Bächen, Bäumen und Bergen, wie mit abgebrochenen Worten auszusprechen sucht. Wen diese einzelnen Laute rühren, der setzt mit wenigen Mitteln die ganze Rede zusammen. *(Ahnung und Gegenwart, SW, III, 101-2)*

Recent criticism has shown quite clearly that it is a mistake to suppose Eichendorff innocent of symbolic intent. Görres' teaching and writings (especially the 1808 essay on Runge's *Die Zeiten)* and the reading of Creuzer and Novalis aroused in him a lively interest in what Görres called 'Hieroglyph der Kunst, plastische Symbolik'. Nature is for Eichendorff, as it had been for Herder, the first hieroglyph, God's manifestation in terms that can, in part at least, be apprehended by man: 'Die Gegend draussen lag unkenntlich und still wie eine wunderbar verschränkte Hieroglyphe im zauberischen Mondschein' *(Das Marmorbild)*. Like the Prague student 'wir studieren unterdes in dem grossen Bilderbuche, das der liebe Gott uns draussen aufgeschlagen hat!' (Chapter Nine). (One is reminded of Wackenroder's chapter 'Von zwei wunderbaren Sprachen' in the *Herzensergiessungen eines kunstliebenden Klosterbruders.)* It is chiefly, however, the poet who is to interpret these hieroglyphs as best he may:

> Das Leben aber... mit seinen bunten Bildern, verhält sich zum Dichter, wie ein unübersehbar weitläufiges Hieroglyphenbuch von einer unbekannten, lange untergegangenen Ursprache zum Leser. Da sitzen von Ewigkeit zu Ewigkeit die redlichsten, gutmütigsten Weltnarren, die Dichter, und lesen und lesen. Aber die alten, wunderbaren Worte der Zeichen sind unbekannt und der Wind weht die Blätter des grossen Buches so schnell und verworren durcheinander, dass einem die Augen übergehn. *(Ahnung und Gegenwart, SW, III, 27)*

Interpretation is not, however, merely a matter of imitating reality:

> Ein solches Übermalen der Natur verwischt vielmehr ihre geheimnisvollen Züge, gleich wie ja auch ein Landschaftsbild nur dadurch zum Kunstwerke wird, dass es die Hieroglyphenschrift, gleichsam

das Lied ohne Worte, und den Geisterblick fühlbar macht, womit die
verborgene Schönheit jeder bestimmten Gegend zu uns reden möchte.
(Poetische Literatur, I, 22)

Nor is nature the only hieroglyph. A secret language having to
do with the condition and purpose of things is spoken by history:

[Kaulbach] ist so recht der Mann dazu, eine ganze historische Idee
mit wenigen Zügen gleichsam hieroglyphisch anzudeuten... (Letter
of 14 November 1853)

church order:

[der] Wunderbau [der Hierarchie], der noch in seiner Erstarrung
hieroglyphisch auf Vergangenheit und Zukunft deutet... *(Die Auf-
hebung der geistlichen Landeshoheit*... (1819) in *Nachlass*, p. 155)

and the religions of the world *(Geschichte des Dramas, p. 2)*.
This testimony, covering most of Eichendorff's adult life, is a
warrant, which should not be abused, for looking below the
surface mood of his work. Finding a depth of meaning in the
Taugenichts is not a perverse intellectual exercise in making
simple matters difficult; it is in harmony with Eichendorff's
own intention. Thus the familiar motifs of Romanticism are
set in a context that invests many of them with symbolic
groupings, and the landscapes, though they seem to be no more
than variations on a limited number of elements, may convey a
whole theology.

Alewyn, in his highly persuasive analysis (1957/60) of a short
landscape description from *Viel Lärmen um Nichts*, argues that
Eichendorff's landscapes are generally unrelated to the context
and that it is quite wrong to think of them as subjective to author
or character. This may be true of the pictorial composition of a
landscape but it is not true of the symbolic values, which, in
the *Taugenichts* at all events, are related to the position of the
hero-narrator. Indeed Alewyn himself later says that space is
Eichendorff's basic landscape experience and that he symbolizes
every possible relationship by spatial values. It is with this in
mind that much of the unconsciously apprehended impact of
the *Taugenichts* on the reader may be understood.

Movement is the main feature of the landscape descriptions.

Straightforward movement of the hero through the world is a compositional technique of the picaresque novel, but here it goes a long way beyond that. At its simplest there is the strong sense of rapid movement in the carriage, conveyed each time in almost identical terms, and in one instance even extended, however inappropriately, to the river-boat:

der Kutscher knallte, und wir flogen über die glänzende Strasse fort, dass mir der Wind am Hute pfiff. Hinter mir gingen nun Dorf, Gärten und Kirchtürme unter... (Chapter One)

Nun ging's, dass mir der Wind am Hute pfiff. Rechts und links flogen Dörfer, Städte und Weingärten vorbei, dass es einem vor den Augen flimmerte... (Chapter Four)

Die Maler sprangen in den Wagen, ich auf den Bock, und so flogen wir schon fort, als eben der Postmeister mit der Schlafmütze aus dem Fenster guckte. (Chapter Four)

bin ich nicht mit ihnen Tag und Nacht fortgereist, zu Pferde und zu Fuss und zu Wagen, dass mir der Wind am Hute pfiff...? (Chapter Seven)

der Schiffer gab das Zeichen, und so flogen wir nun im schönsten Morgenglanze zwischen den Bergen und Wiesen hinunter. (Chapter Nine)

The fixed points, 'Dorf... Gärten... Städte... Weingärten... Kirchtürme... Postmeister/Fenster... Berge... Wiesen' have their static nature emphasized. The Taugenichts has no permanent place in them; his home and his ideal are elsewhere.

The Eichendorff hero is in an equivocal relationship to the world of things. The most notable instance of this is his tendency to isolate himself by climbing a tree, which the Taugenichts does four times. Eichendorff accepted Loeben's criticism of this motif in *Ahnung und Gegenwart*, but he went on using it; and, whether it is an autobiographical reminiscence or a Baroque topos, it apparently also corresponded to some need of the maturer Eichendorff as reflected in his characters. Rising above the general level of nature may be one way of escaping from the problems of its influence.

Eichendorff's general predilection for the view from above has, however, been variously interpreted. Rehder (1957) goes so far as to identify it with the cosmic viewpoint suggested in seventeenth century cosmological and encyclopaedic works and to regard it as a symbol of elevation, of inner sublimity and ecstatic flight as in El Greco. This is perhaps a little too elaborate. The impression one gets is a rather simpler one of breadth of vision and relative detachment, and it is, in fact, almost impossible to separate the view from on high and the distant view. It will be best to take one example to illustrate this:

> Der Weg lief immerfort im Walde an einem Bergeshange fort. Zuweilen konnte man über die Tannenwipfel, die von unten herauflangten und sich dunkel rührten, weit in die tiefen, stillen Täler hinaussehen, hin und her schlug eine Nachtigall, Hunde bellten in der Ferne in den Dörfern. Ein Fluss rauschte beständig aus der Tiefe und blitzte zuweilen im Mondscheine auf. (Chapter Three)

We see here the panoramic stated simply ('lief . . . fort', 'weit . . . hinaus') and reinforced by sound ('Hunde bellten in der Ferne') and by the motion of the river, the landscape element that is continually moving away ('rauschte . . . aus der Tiefe'). The view from above allows the mind's eye to roam ahead of the body (cf. also the last paragraph of Chapter Three: 'Gerade vor uns lag ein unübersehbares Tal . . . Mir war so kühl und fröhlich zumute, als sollt' ich von dem Berge in die prächtige Gegend hinausfliegen'); the depths usually arouse a degree of emotional unease – 'dunkel', 'still', 'blitzen'.

A whole complex of motifs goes to build up the sense of distance, breadth and freedom that is so important for the Taugenichts. Alewyn emphasizes that Eichendorff is not concerned with the infinite landscape, the empty plain or the sea – this is not a Romantic concept at all but one deriving from Sentimentalism or from Idealist philosophy – for in its secularized form infinity is just a euphemism for negation. 'Die Ferne' in Eichendorff, though not attainable, is finite and in the landscape.

The Taugenichts, however, in his alternation of moods, experiences distance as both release and despair. Though indications such as 'fern' and 'weit' emphasize the here that is their reference point – and thus the self standing at the here – they nevertheless suggest the compulsive interplay between that self and the natural world, whatever attempts at withdrawal the individual may make. Distance may draw the self bounding to meet it: 'Ich zeigte bloss auf ein paar Kraniche, die eben hoch über uns durch die Luft zogen, und sagte: Ich müsste nun auch so fort und immer fort, weit in die Ferne!' (Chapter Six). Or it may approach the self through sense-impressions, as in the examples of music from a distance, particularly the *Waldhorn* and the *Posthorn*. In either case the cage of the self is opened.

But distance can also mean disorientation and despair when the connecting lines become too attenuated:

> nicht weit von mir teilte sich die Landstrasse in viele neue Land-strassen, die gingen weit, weit über die höchsten Berge fort, als führten sie aus der Welt hinaus, so dass mir ordentlich schwindelte, wenn ich recht hinsah. (First paragraph of Chapter Three)

'Aus der Welt hinaus' – this is one danger, that of losing the points of reference. The other is that of making the point of reference so remote as to be debarred from proper connexion with the self:

> Ich betrachtete das Firmament, wie da einzelne Wolken langsam durch den Mondschein zogen und manchmal ein Stern weit in der Ferne herunterfiel. So, dachte ich, scheint der Mond auch über meines Vaters Mühle und auf das weisse gräfliche Schloss. Dort ist nun auch schon alles lange still, die gnädige Frau schläft, und die Wasserkünste und Bäume im Garten rauschen noch immerfort wie damals, und allen ist's gleich, ob ich noch da bin, oder in der Fremde, oder gestorben. – Da kam mir die Welt auf einmal so entsetzlich weit und gross vor und ich so ganz allein darin, dass ich aus Herzens-grunde hätte weinen mögen. (Chapter Three)

The world as space, 'die weite Welt', is thus the source of both despair and hope ('Wem Gott will rechte Gunst erweisen, Den schickt er in die weite Welt'). The world as extra-human space, 'die freie Welt', 'Gottes freie Welt' (Chapter One), 'unter Gottes freiem Himmel' (Chapter Eight), is the stage for providential intervening and for temptation and danger. The sense of adventure is inherent in the notion of 'out there', the 'not-self'; once the soul crosses the rim of the self it finds release but also the risk of shipwreck. The Taugenichts is subject, therefore, not merely to the conflicting claims of home and the distant but also to those of the heart and the natural world. Here the heart, a continually recurring reference point, represents the inner home of the self:

Ich war recht im innersten Herzen vergnügt... (Chapter Two)
Ich... grüsste in meinem Herzen die schöne Heimat in der Ferne noch viel tausendmal... (Chapter Seven)

Symbolic of the division between, on the one hand, heart and home and, on the other, nature and distance, is the window. (An obvious example is: 'Es schienen so golden die Sterne, Am Fenster ich einsam stand'). Alewyn claims that the window in Eichendorff is the point of contact between freedom, or life, and prison, or sickness; Hock (1958/60) sees it as '[die] bedeutsame Stelle, wo die festgefügte menschliche Ordnung, der umgrenzte Raum des Hauses, sich öffnet dem unbegrenzten Raum der Landschaft, dem geheimnisvollen Leben der freien Natur'. The symbolic interpretation may be illustrated by a sentence from the second chapter: 'Einmal, als ich eben zu Hause im Fenster liege und verdriesslich in die leere Luft hinaussehe...'; but the most lavish use of the window theme comes in the first chapter. Both the Taugenichts and Aurelie are seen (or not seen) at the window, but the main picture is that of the fair lady behind her window and the suitor behind a bush in flower. At this stage Aurelie seems to live in a self in society and the Taugenichts in a self in nature and they are cut off from each other in these separate environments.

In fact, however, both are in contact with the natural world, with its life-giving and destructive powers. For Eichendorff's nature is not a static object of contemplation. It is active, it moves. Plant-life assumes human attributes, and sometimes there is an animistic confusion of the boundaries between the human body, the spirits and the vegetation:

Aber das war eine liederliche Gärtnerei. Die Gänge waren alle mit hohem Grase gewachsen, die künstlichen Figuren von Buchsbaum waren nicht beschnitten und streckten wie Gespenster lange Nasen oder ellenhohe spitzige Mützen in die Luft hinaus, dass man sich in der Dämmerung ordentlich davor hätte fürchten mögen. (Chapter Six)

... aus allen Sträuchern kam ein Kopf über dem andern hervor, als wenn sie aus der Erde wüchsen. (Chapter Ten)

Kunz (1951) regards the vegetative element as a predominant one in Eichendorff's *Novellen*, though he has reservations in the case of the *Taugenichts* about his unwillingness to develop to the full the tensions between his hero's roots (the plant-like factor) and his new experiences. The externals, Kunz maintains, are significant enough: the Taugenichts as a gardener, his experiences in the Italian gardens, Aurelie's presentation in terms of flowers and the fact that she is in a garden wearing a chaplet of white and red roses when she meets the Taugenichts on his return from Italy. But the essential feature is the parallel between the vegetative dependence on roots and man's attachment to his origins. The plant's goal is always dependent on its beginning, and Aurelie in the garden is equally the still centre of the Taugenichts' roamings. In his return to her he ends where he began.

This is well enough and throws some light on the way the pull of home (for Aurelie subsumes the village, the mill and the dead mother) counteracts the enticement of distance for the Taugenichts. But the vegetative in nature means a good deal more than this and the argument is, indeed, taken a stage further by Schwarz (1957). The Taugenichts, in common with Eichendorff man generally, is subject to two equally strong and valid powers: natural instinct, corresponding to the rhythm of nature or vegetation, and moral obligation. These can only be reunited in Christian love; profane love is powerless to do so, for Venus is herself a vegetative symbol in Eichendorff. (It should here be interpolated that Aurelie seems to embody both sacred and profane love, Venus and the Virgin.)

The rhythmic aspect of man's moods is certainly to be linked with the rhythms of day. Schumann (1936), using the differing emotional reactions to the time of day to illustrate the true

Romanticism of the *Taugenichts*, explains them by the different effects of light and form at various times of the day. But it is by no means clear that Eichendorff's own reactions are as direct as this; his landscapes are more intellectual than sensuously immediate.

The *Taugenichts* opens on an early spring morning and the landscape breathes freedom, freshness and expectancy into the narrative. Morning scenes are always full of hope and new awareness:

> Endlich flogen hin und wieder schon lange, rötliche Scheine über den Himmel, ganz leise, wie wenn man über einen Spiegel haucht, auch eine Lerche sang schon hoch über dem stillen Tale. Da wurde mir auf einmal ganz klar im Herzen bei dem Morgengrusse, und alle Furcht war vorüber. (Chapter Three)

They are not presented realistically but rather as a complex of motifs that acquires almost the status of an allegorical formula. Thus the larks ('die Lerchen schwirren hoch vor Lust', in the first lyric; 'über mir unzählige Lerchen in der klaren, blauen Luft', Chapter One; 'zwischen den Morgenstreifen hoch am Himmel schweiften schon einzelne zu früh erwachte Lerchen', Chapter Two; 'über mir jubilierten unzählige Lerchen hoch in der Luft', last paragraph of Chapter Two; 'hoch in der Luft hörte man manchmal die Lerchen', Chapter Nine) are one of the conventional morning effects of the eighteenth century and of the Romantic writers of the 1810s and 1820s (Arndt, Kerner and Uhland all have poems on the lark), but they also contribute, in the typical language of religion, to a picture of man and nature striving towards heaven. (See also A. Langen, *Der Wortschatz des deutschen Pietismus*, Tübingen, 1954, pp. 198, 472.) This being so, the simile in the German painter's first greeting to the Taugenichts is reinforced: 'Ei, lustiger Gesell, du singst ja wie eine Lerche beim ersten Morgenstrahle!' (Chapter Seven). Similarly the other acoustic effects in these morning passages, such as the cock-crow from the villages around, the postillion blowing his horn and receding into the distance, church bells from afar, birds in the trees, all have their contribution to make to the sense of freedom or adventure.

But one can go further than this and see in the pictures of morning hints of conscious symbolism deriving from Böhme (in Novalis's words: 'In diesem Buche bricht der Morgen/ Gewaltig in die Zeit hinein'), Herder and Runge, or Görres' interpretation of Runge. For Herder (the chapter 'Unter der Morgenröte' in his *Älteste Urkunde des Menschengeschlechts)* every dawn is a hieroglyph of the original creation. Of Runge's *Die Zeiten* Görres wrote in an essay of 1808 (quoted by Möbus, 1954):

> Da steht im Orient tief die Aurora der neuen Zeit... Und es ist Gott selbst, die strahlende Glutensonne der Ewigkeit, die aufgehen will über den Gebirgen, er will lustwandeln in der Frühe und der Kühle, darum haben seine Geister aus dem Saume seiner Herrlichkeit ihm das Blumenparadies gestaltet, und er nähert sich von ferne schon in seiner Glorie...

The morning as the garment of God and the representative of the Creator connects the Taugenichts' wanderings with his spiritual pilgrimage:

> Nur ein früherwachtes Waldvöglein sass vor meinem Fenster auf einem Strauche, der aus der Mauer herauswuchs, und sang schon sein Morgenlied. 'Nein' sagte ich, 'du sollst mich nicht beschämen und allein so früh und fleissig Gott loben!' – Ich nahm schnell meine Geige... und ging hinaus. (Chapter Six)

Yet it should also be noted that he steps straight into a ruined garden, the Eichendorffian home of daemonic powers.

The effect of noon is very different from that of morning. The sun beats down, the air is heavy, life drags along, the heart is filled with foreboding:

> Endlich fing es auch an, sehr schwül zu werden, die Sonnenstrahlen schossen recht wie sengende Pfeile auf das Pflaster, die Leute verkrochen sich in die Häuser, die Jalousien wurden überall wieder zugemacht, und es war auf einmal wie ausgestorben auf den Strassen. Ich warf mich zuletzt ganz verzweifelt vor einem schönen, grossen Hause hin, vor dem ein Balkon mit Säulen breiten Schatten warf, und betrachtete bald die stille Stadt, die in der plötzlichen Einsamkeit bei heller Mittagstunde ordentlich schauerlich aussah, bald wieder

den tiefblauen, ganz wolkenlosen Himmel, bis ich endlich vor grosser
Ermüdung gar einschlummerte. (Chapter Eight)

'Schwül' is a recurrent characteristic: 'an schwülen Nachmitta-
gen' (Chapter One), '[Ich] sass... einmal an einem schwülen
Nachmittage im Wipfel eines hohen Baumes... Die Bienen
summten zwischen den Blättern um mich herum, sonst war
alles wie ausgestorben, kein Mensch war zwischen den Bergen
zu sehen...' (Chapter Six). This again is reminiscent of Görres
on Runge:

> Fern am Gesichtskreis schwebt dreikräftig, ernst, in Geheimnis
> eingehüllt die Gottheit, leise, schwüle Stille geht durch die Natur,
> und sie schaut wie furchtsam zagend auf, denn ihr ist, als ob der
> Unerforschliche zum Zorne sich bewegen wollte.

Midday reveals nature alienated from God.

Evening is bathed in light, the eye is drawn to the far horizons
of the setting sun, sounds carry clearly from great distances, the
rivers run to the sea, and the Taugenichts' moments of greatest
happiness seem to occur then:

> die Sonne ging eben unter und bedeckte das ganze Land mit Glanz
> und Schimmer, die Donau schlängelte sich prächtig wie von lauter
> Gold und Feuer in die weite Ferne, von allen Bergen bis tief ins Land
> hinein sangen und jauchzten die Winzer. Ich... freute mich in der
> lauen Luft, wie der lustige Tag so langsam vor uns verdunkelte und
> verhallte. (Chapter Two)
> Als ich aus dem Gesträuch wieder hervorkroch, neigte sich die Sonne
> zum Untergange. Der Himmel war rot, die Vögel sangen lustig in
> allen Wäldern, die Täler waren voller Schimmer, aber in meinem Her-
> zen war es noch vieltausendmal schöner und fröhlicher. (Chapter Six)

To these must be added the descriptions of the secluded valley
with the idle shepherd in Chapter Three, and the Taugenichts'
return to the castle together with the final love scene. In the
quiet at the day's end the near and the far, the castle and the
Danube are held in balance; the world is wide but not strange,
full of sound but still. In the gold of evening the golden age of
harmony between God, man and the world is, for a while,
restored.

Occasionally evening is regarded as the prelude to night and is associated with its experiences. Guido's song is later called 'Der Abend' but its elements are those of night: 'rauscht die Erde wie in Träumen', 'alte Zeiten, linde Trauer', 'leise Schauer'. Distant sounds are heard again – the barking of dogs, the song of the nightingale, the fountains, distant rivers: '. . . hin und her schlug eine Nachtigall, Hunde bellten in der Ferne in den Dörfern. Ein Fluss rauschte beständig aus der Tiefe und blitzte zuweilen im Mondscheine auf' (Chapter Three). Moonlight is the constant feature and its effect is plain in the continuation of the above passage. Also accompanies other moments of tension, confusion and unease: the lightning playing round the glimpse of the hunch-backed devil figure; the eerie ride in the carriage to the Italian castle ('ein wüstes Gebirge mit grauen Schluchten', 'der Mond. . . schien auf einmal so hell zwischen die Bäume und Felsen herein, dass es ordentlich grauslich anzusehen war', 'als führen wir in ein grosses Grabgewölbe hinein') and the subsequent dream ('Es kam mir vor, als führe ich noch immerfort im Wagen, und es hätte mir von einem Schlosse im Mondscheine geträumt und von einer alten Hexe mit ihrem blassen Töchterlein', first paragraph of Chapter Six); the shadow of the Taugenichts on the heath; the painter in the Roman garden ('Er sprach noch immerfort und war dabei mit seinen verwirrten Haaren von dem Tanzen und Trinken im Mondscheine ganz leichenblass anzusehen', Chapter Eight). But the moon wears a double aspect; it shines too on the gates and cupolas of Rome, 'als ständen wirklich die Engel in goldenen Gewändern auf den Zinnen und sängen durch die stille Nacht herüber' (Chapter Seven) and on the home of the Taugenichts and Aurelie – 'siehst du. . . das weisse Schlösschen, das da drüben im Mondscheine glänzt, das hat uns der Graf geschenkt . . . da werden wir wohnen'. Night can bring peace and harmony by deadening the distinctions between things and showing the unity of the world; but it can also, because of its mysteries, suggest the daemonic in man and in the natural world.

In this respect it is like the forest: 'Wir müssen, dachte ich, doch am Ende aus dem Walde und aus der Nacht kommen'. The woods are silent and lonely ('niemand zu sehen', 'kein Laut zu vernehmen', 'in dem einsamen Walde') and in them man can retreat into himself and see life entire; but they are also the old homes of the gods, mysterious and vaguely threatening: 'mir fing beinahe an angst zu werden in dem ewigen einsamen Rauschen der Wälder' (Chapter Three). *Waldeinsamkeit* represents both tranquillity and foreboding.

From what has been said hitherto it will be clear that the *Taugenichts* contains many symbolic patterns that are part of a semi-allegorical general structure. The work is not merely a delightful exercise in fantasy; it is also part of Eichendorff's attempt to formulate a theology of nature or landscape. That it is a more hopeful approach than in *Ahnung und Gegenwart* or *Das Marmorbild* explains the predominance of some of the symbolic patterns (for example, morning and evening) and the mere hinting at others, such as Venus.

The *Taugenichts* is, of course, not a fully developed religious allegory, but it may be useful to make a semi-allegorical summary of it. This would run something like this:

Christian, the Taugenichts, whose vision is not purely purposive but has in it something of the freedom of the artist, is drawn from the safety but also the limitations of his home (his roots) by the attraction of ideal distance (the temporal world in its beauty). There is peril for him in the unredeemed world (that of Venus, heaths and heathens, lost cities, ruined gardens, ghostly trees, the heat of noon); it is the realm of transience and of the purely sensual. Yet the natural world can also be the instrument of providence; its woods at night may be frightening but they may also cause Christian to sink into God's arms. And in the morning the world is redeemed and reborn.

Ideal distance is chiefly represented by Italy, the beautiful enchantress with all her memorials to the transient. But Rome is also the holy city and in memory it is linked with the Taugenichts' childhood home. Heaven and home are joined; 'in my beginning is my end'.

The strongest force drawing him home (for his country, too, is his home) is the non-sensual, quasi-sacred love he bears Aurelie, the virginal (and Virginlike), though even she in his dream has at one stage threatened to modulate into the temptress Venus. The church, the Stephansturm and the old priest, both welcome him and assist him in his return; and the world of appearance (the disguises and the misunderstandings) fades before the touch of reality. Christian is accepted into a community; he is placed in his own private Eden with the commandment to 'be fruitful and multiply' (though the rabbit simile takes any portentousness away from the notion). Enfolded in Aurelie's love he can even think of returning to Italy, but this time in the company of the porter, symbol of reality, and the Prague students, symbols of a more directed wandering. The *Novelle* ends in the garden with the Danube, the river of life, flowing on. And, in the formula of Creation, 'Behold, it was very good'.

Aus dem Leben eines Taugenichts employs many romantic motifs and embodies many romantic attitudes; its details sometimes herald the bourgeois parochialism of minor Biedermeier writers; its use of symbols in a semi-allegorical framework links it both with the conscious effects of the early Romantic writers and with the less explicit symbolism of the later realists. But the *Taugenichts* as a *Novelle*, and the Taugenichts himself, cannot be confined within some neatly labelled room. They are not samples from the storehouse of some literary school, but the comments of a poet on man's estate. The *Taugenichts* is an optimistic work. The narrative tone is such that innocence prevails. The shadows and temptations of life are no more than hinted at.

But the high seriousness of the poet Eichendorff is still apparent. Though the estrangement from nature, the loss of paradise, are overcome by providential care, the condition of man has still been called in question. The Taugenichts himself is man stripped to his essentials – disinterested, unencumbered, 'good-for-nothing' except to be God's creature.

This, then, is the German Pilgrim's progress.

Select Bibliography

A. TEXTS

(There is, as yet, no generally acceptable text of *Aus dem Leben eines Taugenichts*, though this should be remedied when volume V (*Märchen und Novellen*, ed. H. Kunisch) of the critical edition appears. The other volumes of this edition, *Sämtliche Werke*, ed.W. Kosch and A. Sauer, Regensburg, 1908 ff., are quoted as *SW*, I, etc.

The edition of the *Taugenichts* quoted, with some modifications, is that of A. Müller in *Phantasiestücke* (= Deutsche Literatur ... in Entwicklungs-reihen, Reihe Romantik, XVIII), Leipzig, 1936, pp. 218-97 and, notes, 312-4).

Aus dem Leben eines Taugenichts, facsimile of the first MS draft, ed. A. Jahn, Neisse, [1939], 20 pp., 700 no. copies.

Scènes de la vie d'un propre à rien (= Collection bilingue des classiques étrangers), ed. P. Sucher, Paris, 1929, xl + 116 double pages + pp. 117-20; new ed., Paris, 1941.

Memoirs of a good-for-nothing, transl. B. Q. Morgan, London, 1955, viii + 120 pp.

Werke und Schriften, neue Gesamtausgabe, ed. G. Baumann and S. Grosse, Stuttgart, 1957-8, 4 vols. (*Aus dem Leben eines Taugenichts*, II, 349-434; 'Der neue Troubadour', IV, 1493-1511).

Vermischte Schriften, Paderborn, 1866, containing *Geschichte der poetischen Literatur Deutschlands*, 3rd ed., *Der deutsche Roman des 18. Jahrhunderts*, 2nd ed., *Zur Geschichte des Dramas*, 2nd ed., and *Aus dem literarischen Nachlasse*.

B. STUDIES OF 'AUS DEM LEBEN EINES TAUGENICHTS'

E. P. Appelt, 'Selbsterlebtes in Eichendorffs *Aus dem Leben eines Tauge-nichts*', *Philological Quarterly*, VII, 1928, 275-82.

Friedrich G. Bauer, 'Die Gedichteinlagen in Eichendorffs Novelle *Aus dem Leben eines Taugenichts*', *Monatshefte für deutschen Unterricht*, XXV, 1933, 139-48.

Chester Nathan Gould, 'Literary Satire in Eichendorff's Novelle *Aus dem Leben eines Taugenichts*', *Journal of English and Germanic Philology*, XXXIII, 1934, 167-77.

Ernst Feise, 'Eichendorffs *Aus dem Leben eines Taugenichts*', *Monatshefte für deutschen Unterricht*, XXVIII, 1936, 8-16; and in his *Xenion. Themes, forms and ideas in German literature*, Baltimore, 1950, pp. 123-34.

Detlev W. Schumann, 'Eichendorff's *Taugenichts* and Romanticism', *German Quarterly*, IX, 1936, 141-53.

Amalie Bosselmann-Franzen, 'Die Bedeutung der Gestalt des Taugenichts in Eichendorffs *Aus dem Leben eines Taugenichts*', *Monatshefte für deutschen Unterricht*, XXXI, 1939, 265-73.

Joachim Müller, 'Eichendorffs Erzählung *Aus dem Leben eines Taugenichts*', *Zeitschrift für Deutschkunde*, LIV, 1940, 66-70.

J. D. Workman, 'The significance of the Taugenichts for Eichendorff', *Monatshefte für deutschen Unterricht*, XXXIII, 1941, 64-76.

Maria Bindschedler, 'Der Taugenichts', *Neue Schweizer Rundschau*, XI, 1943, 364-70.

Oskar Seidlin, 'Der Taugenichts ante portas. Interpretation einer Eichendorff-Stelle', *Journal of English and Germanic Philology*, LII, 1953, 509-24; and in *Aurora*, XVI, 1956, 70-81.

Richard Stecher, *Erläuterungen zu Eichendorffs Aus dem Leben eines Taugenichts* (= Dr.Wilhelm Königs Erläuterungen zu den Klassikern, 215), 3rd ed., Hollfeld/Obfr., [1955], 63 pp.

Benno vonWiese, 'Joseph von Eichendorff – Aus dem Leben eines Taugenichts', in *Die deutsche Novelle von Goethe bis Kafka: Interpretationen*, Düsseldorf, 1956, pp. 79-96.

Josef Ruland, 'Eichendorffs *Taugenichts* and J. J. Rousseaus *Confessions*', *Zeitschrift für deutsche Philologie*, LXXV, 1956, 375-85.

Egon Schwarz, 'Der Taugenichts zwischen Heimat und Exil', *Études Germaniques*, XII, 1957, 18-33.

C. GENERAL CRITICISM

Lorenzo Bianchi, *Italien in Eichendorffs Dichtung. Eine Untersuchung*, Bologna, 1937, 139 pp.

Gisela Jahn, *Studien zu Eichendorffs Prosastil* (= Palaestra, 206), Leipzig, 1937, x + 129 pp.

RenéWehrli, *Eichendorffs Erlebnis und Gestaltung der Sinnenwelt* (= Wege zur Dichtung, 32), Frauenfeld & Leipzig, 1938, 279 pp.

Wilhelm Emrich, 'Eichendorff. Skizze einer Ästhetik der Geschichte', *Germanisch-Romanische Monatsschrift*, XXVII, 1939, 192-207.

Regina Häusler, *Das Bild Italiens in der deutschen Romantik* (= Sprache und Dichtung, 63), Bern & Leipzig, 1939, xii + 141 pp.

Georg Lukács, 'Eichendorff', an essay dated 1940 in his *Deutsche Realisten des 19. Jahrhunderts*, Berlin, 1952, pp. 49-65.

Rudolf Ibel, *Weltschau deutscher Dichter*, Hamburg, 1948; new ed., Frankfurt a.M., Berlin & Bonn, [1958], Eichendorff pp. 49-97 and 205-8.

Werner Kohlschmidt, 'Die symbolische Formelhaftigkeit von Eichendorffs Prosastil', *Orbis litterarum*, VIII, 1950, 322-54; and in his *Form und Innerlichkeit*, Bern, 1955, pp. 177-209.

Josef Kunz, *Eichendorff. Höhepunkt und Krise der Spätromantik*, Oberursel, 1951, 253 pp.

Otto Keller, *Eichendorffs Kritik der Romantik*, Zürich, 1954, 83 pp. (Diss., Zürich).

Gerhard Möbus, *Eichendorff in Heidelberg* (= Deutscher Osten, 14), Düsseldorf, 1954, 127 pp.

Ernst Scheyer, 'Eichendorff und die bildenden Künste', *Aurora*, XVI, 1956, 7-33.

Richard Alewyn, 'Eine Landschaft Eichendorffs', *Euphorion*, LI, 1957, 42-60; and in *Eichendorff Heute*, ed. P. Stöcklein, München, 1960, pp. 19-43.

Helmut Rehder, 'Ursprünge dichterischer Emblematik in Eichendorffs Prosawerken', *Journal of English and Germanic Philology*, LVI, 1957, 528–41.

Oskar Seidlin, 'Eichendorff's Symbolic Landscape', *Publications of the Modern Language Association of America*, LXXII, 1957, 645–61; and in *Eichendorff Heute*, supra, 1960, pp. 218–41.

Erich Hock, 'Eichendorffs Dichtertum', *Wirkendes Wort*, VIII, 1958, 155–66; and in *Eichendorff Heute*, supra, 1960, pp. 106–23.

Leo Spitzer, 'Zu einer Landschaft Eichendorffs', *Euphorion*, LII, 1958, 142–52.

Gerhard Möbus, *Der andere Eichendorff*, Osnabrück, 1960, 206 pp.

D. BIOGRAPHY

Hans Brandenburg, *Joseph von Eichendorff. Sein Leben und sein Werk*, München, 1922, xii + 531 pp.

Willibald Köhler, *Joseph von Eichendorff. Ein Dichterleben in 11 Kapiteln*, Augsburg, 1957, 280 pp.

E. BIBLIOGRAPHY

Karl Freiherr von Eichendorff, *Ein Jahrhundert Eichendorff-Literatur* (= *Sämtliche Werke*, ed.W. Kosch, XXII), Regensburg, [1927], viii + 160 pp.

Wolfgang Kron, 'Eichendorff-Bibliographie', in *Eichendorff Heute*, supra, 1960, pp. 280–329 (excellent).